OpenStack Trove Essentials

Build your own cloud based Database as a Service using OpenStack Trove

Alok Shrivastwa

Sunil Sarat

BIRMINGHAM - MUMBAI

OpenStack Trove Essentials

First published: March 2016

Production reference: 1220316

Published by Packt Publishing Ltd.
Livery Place
35 Livery Street
Birmingham B3 2PB, UK.

ISBN 978-1-78528-561-5

www.packtpub.com

Credits

Authors
Alok Shrivastwa
Sunil Sarat

Reviewer
Denys Makogon

Commissioning Editor
Dipika Gaonkar

Acquisition Editor
Rahul Nair

Content Development Editor
Viranchi Shetty

Technical Editor
Nirant Carvalho

Copy Editors
Jonathan Todd
Madhusudan Uchil

Project Coordinator
Izzat Contractor

Proofreader
Safis Editing

Indexer
Hemangini Bari

Graphics
Kirk D'Penha

Production Coordinator
Shantanu N. Zagade

Cover Work
Shantanu N. Zagade

About the Authors

Alok Shrivastwa is a technologist from India, currently working as the director of cloud services for Microland Ltd. in their Center of Innovation. He has a keen interest in all things physical and metaphysical and is an innovator at heart. He has worked with multiple large- and medium-sized enterprises, designing and implementing their network security solutions, automation solutions, databases, VoIP environments, datacenter designs, public and private clouds, and integrations.

He has also created several tools and intellectual properties in the field of operationalization of emerging technologies. He has authored a book, *Learning OpenStack*, with Packt Publishing, and has authored several whitepapers and blogs on technology and metaphysical topics, in addition to writing poems in Hindi. Also, he has been a guest speaker for undergraduate engineering students in Chennai.

You can connect with him at `https://in.linkedin.com/in/alokas` or follow him on Twitter at `@alok_as`.

We are like the fire at the end of the matchstick, we appear when we are needed, and once our work here is completed, we disappear into the same nothingness we all came from. I thank that nothingness we all fondly call God. I thank my mother, Seema, for making me who I am today; my lovely sisters, Kawshiki and Abhabya; my beautiful wife, Priyanka, for tolerating the insanity; and my father for supporting me throughout.

I thank the reviewers who were patient in reviewing the work and shaped the flow of the book. I thank all the editors at Packt for being extremely helpful and understanding and finally Packt Publishing for allowing me to share whatever little I know.

Sunil Sarat is the vice president of cloud and mobility services at Microland Ltd., an India-based global hybrid IT infrastructure services provider.

He played a key role in setting up and running the emerging technologies practice, dealing with areas such as public/private cloud (AWS and Azure, VMware vCloud Suite, Microsoft, and OpenStack), hybrid IT (VMware vRealize automation/ orchestration, Chef, and Puppet), enterprise mobility (Citrix Xenmobile and VMware Airwatch), VDI /app virtualization (VMware Horizon Suite, Citrix XenDesktop/ XenApp, Microsoft RDS, and AppV), and associated transformation services.

He is a technologist and a business leader with expertise in creating new practices and service portfolios, building and managing high-performance teams, strategy definition, technological roadmaps, and 24/7 global remote infrastructure operations. He has varied experience in handling diverse functions such as innovation/technology, service delivery, transition, presales/solutions, and automation.

He has authored whitepapers, blogs, and articles on various technologies and service-related areas, is a speaker at cloud-related events, and reviews technical books. He has authored *Learning OpenStack* and reviewed *Learning AirWatch* and *Mastering VMware Horizon 6*, all by Packt Publishing.

He holds various industry certifications in the areas of compute, storage, and security and holds an MBA in marketing.

Besides technology and business, he is passionate about filmmaking and is a part-time filmmaker as well.

For more information, you can visit his LinkedIn profile at https://www.linkedin. com/in/sunilsarat or follow him on Twitter at @sunilsarat.

Firstly, I would like to thank the Existence for enabling me to write this book. I would like to thank my family — my mother, Ratna; wife, Abhaya; and my twins, Advika and Agnika — for supporting me throughout. Thanks to my friends Karthieyan K., Syed, Samina, and Mayank for their encouragement.

I thank Microland for all the exposure and support provided, which was instrumental for me to write this book. My gratitude to my co-author Alok Shrivastwa and, last but not least, to Packt Publishing for the opportunity and guidance.

About the Reviewer

Denys Makogon is a senior Python software engineer at EPAM and works in Kharkiv, Ukraine. He is a writer and developer by day and a reader by night. His passion is helping people bring their technical skills up to the next level along with developing skills that would become key features in obtaining a story of success for both sides—developers and customers. He is an IT "tough guy", cloud-native application developer, and has started work as a software architect in cloud-based solutions. He is the founder of the Project Invader open source organization, mainly focused on developing and designing platform and software as a service applications for OpenStack. He is a contributor to the OpenStack DBaaS and the CloudValidation open source framework. He is a founder and technical project lead of the BeeDB project. He has worked on *OpenStack Cloud Applications Development* (`http://as.wiley.com/WileyCDA/WileyTitle/productCd-1119194318.html`).

I would like to say thank you to the entire team that helped me get the work done in time and at an appropriate level and supported me within this project and to my family that helped me stay concentrated on this book.

www.PacktPub.com

eBooks, discount offers, and more

Did you know that Packt offers eBook versions of every book published, with PDF and ePub files available? You can upgrade to the eBook version at www.PacktPub.com and as a print book customer, you are entitled to a discount on the eBook copy. Get in touch with us at customercare@packtpub.com for more details.

At www.PacktPub.com, you can also read a collection of free technical articles, sign up for a range of free newsletters and receive exclusive discounts and offers on Packt books and eBooks.

https://www2.packtpub.com/books/subscription/packtlib

Do you need instant solutions to your IT questions? PacktLib is Packt's online digital book library. Here, you can search, access, and read Packt's entire library of books.

Why subscribe?

- Fully searchable across every book published by Packt
- Copy and paste, print, and bookmark content
- On demand and accessible via a web browser

Table of Contents

Preface

Database management has come a long way over the last decade or so. The process of provisioning databases used to start with racking and stacking a physical server, installing and configuring an operating system, and finally, installing and configuring a database management system. This entire process took weeks and, in some cases, months. Once the database is provisioned, you then of course have a whole host of things to be managed, including availability, backups, security, and performance. This provisioning and management consumed a lot of time and resources. During the evolution, we had two trends that have had a significant impact on the way databases were provisioned and managed. Automation eased the management aspect and virtualization eased the provisioning, at least up to the operating-system layer. Meanwhile, the other trend that we have seen is that enterprises are moving away from a single database technology model to a model which is fancily termed "polyglot persistence". This basically means adopting multiple database technologies with the intention of storing the data in a database that is best suited for that type of data. With multiple types of database technologies coming into play, enterprises are finding it difficult to manage this complexity while maintaining corporate standards and compliance.

Fortunately for us, over the last couple of years, cloud is the other trend that came to our rescue. With the advent of cloud, we have initially seen self-service based agile provisioning of infrastructure take off, which has been termed as Infrastructure as a Service and has automated a lot of aspects and made infrastructure management easier. Building on this a bit more, we now have self-service based agile provisioning of multiple types of databases, which is popularly known as Database as a Service (DBaaS). This has made things much easier for enterprises in terms of bringing in efficiencies and enforcing corporate standards and compliance. Enterprises can avail DBaaS from a public cloud such as Amazon Web Services or Microsoft Azure. Alternatively, they can build their own private cloud-based DBaaS and the need for this could be owing to various reasons such as data privacy and security. This is where OpenStack and Trove comes into the picture. OpenStack Trove is an open source implementation of DBaaS. While it has been in existence for a couple of years, it has started gaining momentum only recently with enterprises giving it a serious thought.

The benefits of DBaaS in general and OpenStack Trove in particular are obvious. The key challenge, however, is that beyond the documentation that is available from the OpenStack project itself, there is not much reading material out there to help potential DBAs and system/cloud administrators. This lack of skill and know-how is one of the potential inhibitors to OpenStack Trove adoption.

This book is an attempt to provide all the essential information that is necessary to kick-start your learning of OpenStack Trove and set up your own cloud-based DBaaS. In this book, the readers will be introduced to all major components of OpenStack Trove. Following this, the readers will get to understand how to set up Trove in both development and production environments, configuring it, and performing management activities such as backup and restore. Not to mention, it also deals with certain advanced database features, such as replication and clustering. This book takes a more practical approach to learning, as the learning from each chapter will contribute to the reader's ability to build his/her own private cloud-based DBaaS by the time he/she completes reading this book. We hope you will enjoy reading this book and, more importantly, find it useful in your journey towards learning and implementing DBaaS using OpenStack Trove.

What this book covers

Chapter 1, Introducing OpenStack Trove, introduces the concept of Database as a Service and its advantages, followed by a quick introduction to the OpenStack Trove project and its components.

Chapter 2, Setting up Trove with DevStack in a Box, provides a list of prerequisites for the book. This chapter also helps you understand DevStack and its components and then helps you set up Trove with DevStack.

Chapter 3, Installing Trove in an Existing OpenStack Environment, gives you an overview of the different available methods to deploy Trove. It deals a little bit more in detail with installing Trove from source and the Ubuntu repository.

Chapter 4, Preparing the Guest Images, as the name implies, details how to build production-ready images that will be required by Trove.

Chapter 5, Provisioning Database Instances, looks at creating and launching instances using both CLI and GUI.

Chapter 6, Configuring the Trove Instances, introduces you to configuring Trove instances and also how to make configuration changes to multiple Trove instances using configuration groups.

Chapter 7, Database Backup and Restore, introduces the concept of Strategies and provides an overview of how to back up and restore Trove instances.

Chapter 8, Advanced Database Features, deals with advanced features such as replication and clustering in Trove.

What you need for this book

For all the chapters, you will require Ubuntu system and DevStack installed.

Who this book is for

This book is intended for database administrators having experience with RDBMS and NoSQL databases wanting to offer DBaaS (short for Database as a Service) to the end users using OpenStack Trove. It assumes that the readers have experience in database administration with one or more databases, preferably with MySQL

This book will help any reader trying to build their skills in OpenStack Trove. We believe that this is the right kind of opportunity for all those of you who have embarked on a journey to build OpenStack Trove skills and enhance your career in the next generation cloud world

Conventions

In this book, you will find a number of text styles that distinguish between different kinds of information. Here are some examples of these styles and an explanation of their meaning.

Code words in text, database table names, folder names, filenames, file extensions, pathnames, dummy URLs, user input, and Twitter handles are shown as follows: "We should be able to find the screen name using the `screen -ls` command."

A block of code is set as follows:

```
FLOATING_RANGE=192.168.1.0/27
FIXED_RANGE=10.1.10.0/24
FIXED_NETWORK_SIZE=256
FLAT_INTERFACE=eth0
ADMIN_PASSWORD=adm1npwd
DATABASE_PASSWORD=dbr00tpwd
RABBIT_PASSWORD=rabb1tpwd
SERVICE_PASSWORD=oss3rvice
SERVICE_TOKEN=x1y1z1token
```

Any command-line input or output is written as follows:

```
export http_proxy=http://172.21.2.17:80
export https_proxy=http://172.21.2.17:80
export no_proxy=localhost,172.22.6.0/24
```

New terms and **important words** are shown in bold. Words that you see on the screen, for example, in menus or dialog boxes, appear in the text like this: "Once you are able to log in, navigate to **System | System Information**."

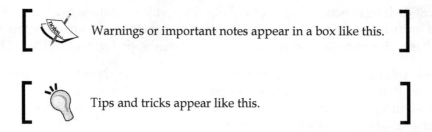

Warnings or important notes appear in a box like this.

Tips and tricks appear like this.

Reader feedback

Feedback from our readers is always welcome. Let us know what you think about this book—what you liked or disliked. Reader feedback is important for us as it helps us develop titles that you will really get the most out of.

To send us general feedback, simply e-mail `feedback@packtpub.com`, and mention the book's title in the subject of your message.

If there is a topic that you have expertise in and you are interested in either writing or contributing to a book, see our author guide at `www.packtpub.com/authors`.

Customer support

Now that you are the proud owner of a Packt book, we have a number of things to help you to get the most from your purchase.

Errata

Although we have taken every care to ensure the accuracy of our content, mistakes do happen. If you find a mistake in one of our books—maybe a mistake in the text or the code—we would be grateful if you could report this to us. By doing so, you can save other readers from frustration and help us improve subsequent versions of this book. If you find any errata, please report them by visiting `http://www.packtpub.com/submit-errata`, selecting your book, clicking on the **Errata Submission Form** link, and entering the details of your errata. Once your errata are verified, your submission will be accepted and the errata will be uploaded to our website or added to any list of existing errata under the Errata section of that title.

To view the previously submitted errata, go to `https://www.packtpub.com/books/content/support` and enter the name of the book in the search field. The required information will appear under the **Errata** section.

Piracy

Piracy of copyrighted material on the Internet is an ongoing problem across all media. At Packt, we take the protection of our copyright and licenses very seriously. If you come across any illegal copies of our works in any form on the Internet, please provide us with the location address or website name immediately so that we can pursue a remedy.

Please contact us at copyright@packtpub.com with a link to the suspected pirated material.

We appreciate your help in protecting our authors and our ability to bring you valuable content.

Questions

If you have a problem with any aspect of this book, you can contact us at questions@packtpub.com, and we will do our best to address the problem.

1
Introducing OpenStack Trove

OpenStack Trove truly and remarkably is a treasure or collection of valuable things, especially for open source lovers like us and, of course, it is an apt name for the **Database as a Service (DBaaS)** component of OpenStack. In this book, we shall see why this component shows the potential and is on its way to becoming one of the crucial components in the OpenStack world.

In this chapter, we will cover the following:

- DBaaS and its advantages
- An introduction to OpenStack's Trove project and its components

Database as a Service

Data is a key component in today's world, and what would applications do without data? Data is very critical, especially in the case of businesses such as the financial sector, social media, e-commerce, healthcare, and streaming media. Storing and retrieving data in a manageable way is absolutely key. Databases, as we all know, have been helping us manage data for quite some time now.

Databases form an integral part of any application. Also, the data-handling needs of different type of applications are different, which has given rise to an increase in the number of database types. As the overall complexity increases, it becomes increasingly challenging and difficult for the **database administrators (DBAs)** to manage them.

DBaaS is a cloud-based service-oriented approach to offering databases on demand for storing and managing data. DBaaS offers a flexible and scalable platform that is oriented towards self-service and easy management, particularly in terms of provisioning a business' environment using a database of choice in a matter of a few clicks and in minutes rather than waiting on it for days or even, in some cases, weeks.

The fundamental building block of any DBaaS is that it will be deployed over a cloud platform, be it public (AWS, Azure, and so on) or private (VMware, OpenStack, and so on). In our case, we are looking at a private cloud running OpenStack. So, to the extent necessary, you might come across references to OpenStack and its other services, on which Trove depends.

XaaS (short for **Anything/Everything as a Service**, of which DBaaS is one such service) is fast gaining momentum. In the cloud world, everything is offered as a service, be it infrastructure, software, or, in this case, databases. **Amazon Web Services** (**AWS**) offers various services around this: the **Relational Database Service** (**RDS**) for the **RDBMS** (short for **relational database management system**) kind of system; **SimpleDB** and **DynamoDB** for NoSQL databases; and **Redshift** for data warehousing needs.

The OpenStack world was also not untouched by the growing demand for DBaaS, not just by users but also by DBAs, and as a result, Trove made its debut with the OpenStack release Icehouse in April 2014 and since then is one of the most popular advanced services of OpenStack.

It supports several SQL and NoSQL databases and provides the full life cycle management of the databases.

Advantages

Now, you must be wondering why we must even consider DBaaS over traditional database management strategies. Here are a few points you might want to consider that might make it worth your time.

Reduced database management costs

In any organization, most of their DBAs' time is wasted in mundane tasks such as creating databases, creating instances, and so on. They are not able to concentrate on tasks such as fine-tuning SQL queries so that applications run faster, not to mention the time taken to do it all manually (or with a bunch of scripts that need to be fired manually), so this in effect is wasting resources in terms of both developers' and DBAs' time. This can be significantly reduced using a DBaaS.

Faster provisioning and standardization

With DBaaS, databases that are provisioned by the system will be compliant with standards as there is very little human intervention involved. This is especially helpful in the case of heavily regulated industries. As an example, let's look at members of the healthcare industry. They are bound by regulations such as **HIPAA** (short for **Health Insurance Portability and Accountability Act** of 1996), which enforces certain controls on how data is to be stored and managed. Given this scenario, DBaaS makes the database provisioning process easy and compliant as they only need to qualify the process once, and then every other database coming out of the automated provisioning system is then compliant with the standards or controls set.

Easier administration

Since DBaaS is cloud based, which means there will be a lot of automation, administration becomes that much more automated and easier. Some important administration tasks are backup/recovery and software upgrade/downgrade management. As an example, with most databases, we should be able to push configuration modifications within minutes to all the database instances that have been spun out by the DBaaS system. This ensures that any new standards being thought of can easily be implemented.

Scaling and efficiency

Scaling (up or down) becomes immensely easy, and this reduces resource hogging, which developers used as part of their planning for a rainy day, and in most cases, it never came. In the case of DBaaS, since you don't commit resources upfront and only scale up or down as and when necessary, resource utilization will be highly efficient.

These are some of the advantages available to organizations that use DBaaS. Some of the concerns and roadblocks for organizations in adopting DBaaS, especially in a public cloud model, are as follows:

- Companies don't want to have sensitive data leave their premises.
- Database access and speed are key to application performance. Not being able to manage the underlying infrastructure inhibits some organizations from going to a DBaaS model.

In contrast to public cloud-based DBaaS, concerns regarding data security, performance, and visibility reduce significantly in the case of private DBaaS systems such as Trove. In addition, the benefits of a cloud environment are not lost either.

Trove

OpenStack Trove, which was originally called **Red Dwarf**, is a project that was initiated by HP, and many others contributed to it later on, including Rackspace. The project was in incubation till the Havana release of OpenStack.

It was formally introduced in the Icehouse release in April 2014, and its mission is to provide scalable and reliable cloud DBaaS provisioning functionality for relational and non-relational database engines.

As of the Liberty release, Trove is considered as a **big-tent** service.

Big-tent is a new approach that allows projects to enter the OpenStack code namespace. In order for a service to be a big-tent service, it only needs to follow some basic rules, which are listed here. This allows the projects to have access to the shared teams in OpenStack, such as the infrastructure teams, release management teams, and documentation teams. The project should:

- Align with the OpenStack mission
- Subject itself to the rulings of the OpenStack Technical Committee
- Support Keystone authentication
- Be completely open source and open community based

At the time of writing this book, the adoption and maturity levels are as shown here:

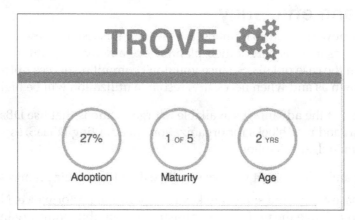

The previous diagram shows that the **Age** of the project is just **2 YRS** and it has a **27% Adoption** rate, meaning 27 of 100 people running OpenStack also run Trove.

The maturity index is **1** on a scale of 1 to 5. It is derived from the following five aspects:

- The presence of an installation guide
- Whether the **Adoption** percentage is greater or lesser than 75
- Stable branches of the project
- Whether it supports seven or more SDKs
- Corporate diversity in the team working on the project

Without further ado, let's take a look at the architecture that Trove implements in order to provide DBaaS.

Architecture

The trove project uses some shared components and some dedicated project-related components as mentioned in the following subsections.

Shared components

The Trove system shares two components with the other OpenStack projects: the backend database (MySQL/MariaDB), and the message bus.

The message bus

The **AMQP** (short for **Advanced Message Queuing Protocol**) message bus brokers the interactions between the task manager, API, guest agent, and conductor. This component ensures that Trove can be installed and configured as a distributed system.

MySQL/MariaDB

MySQL or MariaDB is used by Trove to store the state of the system.

API

This component is responsible for providing the RESTful API with JSON and XML support. This component can be called the face of Trove to the external world since all the other components talk to Trove using this. It talks to the task manager for complex tasks, but it can also talk to the guest agent directly to perform simple tasks, such as retrieving users.

The task manager

The task manager is the engine responsible for doing the majority of the work. It is responsible for provisioning instances, managing the life cycle, and performing different operations. The task manager normally sends common commands, which are of an abstract nature; it is the responsibility of the guest agent to read them and issue database-specific commands in order to execute them.

The guest agent

The guest agent runs inside the Nova instances that are used to run the database engines. The agent listens to the messaging bus for the topic and is responsible for actually translating and executing the commands that are sent to it by the task manager component for the particular datastore.

Let's also look at the different types of guest agents that are required depending on the database engine that needs to be supported. The different guest agents (for example, the MySQL and PostgreSQL guest agents) may even have different capabilities depending on what is supported on the particular database. This way, different datastores with different capabilities can be supported, and the system is kept extensible.

The conductor

The conductor component is responsible for updating the Trove backend database with the information that the guest agent sends regarding the instances. It eliminates the need for direct database access by all the guest agents for updating information. This is like the way the guest agent also listens to the topic on the messaging bus and performs its functions based on it.

The following diagram can be used to illustrate the different components of Trove and also their interaction with the dependent services:

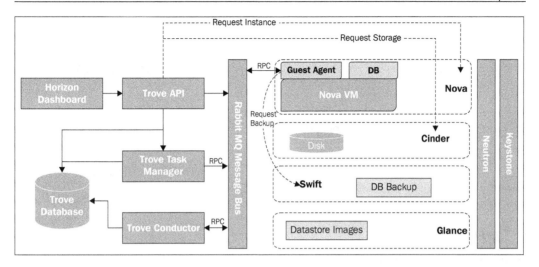

Terminology

Let's take a look at some of the terminology that Trove uses.

Datastore

Datastore is the term used for the RDBMS or NoSQL database that Trove can manage; it is nothing more than an abstraction of the underlying database engine, for example, MySQL, MongoDB, Percona, Couchbase, and so on.

Datastore version

This is linked to the datastore and defines a set of packages to be installed or already installed on an image. As an example, let's take MySQL 5.5. The datastore version will also link to a base image (operating system) that is stored in Glance.

The configuration parameters that can be modified are also dependent on the datastore and the datastore version.

Instance

An instance is an instantiation of a datastore version. It runs on OpenStack Nova and uses Cinder for persistent storage. It has a full OS and additionally has the guest agent of Trove.

Configuration group

A configuration group is a bunch of options that you can set. As an example, we can create a group and associate a number of instances to one configuration group, thereby maintaining the configurations in sync.

Flavor

The flavor is similar to the Nova machine flavor, but it is just a definition of memory and CPU requirements for the instance that will run and host the databases.

Normally, it's a good idea to have a high memory-to-CPU ratio as a flavor for running database instances.

Database

This is the actual database that the users consume. Several databases can run in a single Trove instance. This is where the actual users or applications connect with their database clients.

The following diagram shows these different terminologies, as a quick summary. Users or applications connect to databases, which reside in instances. The instances run in Nova but are instantiations of the **Datastore version** belonging to a **Datastore**. Just to explain this a little further, say we have two versions of MySQL that are being serviced. We will have one datastore but two datastore versions, and any instantiation of that will be called an instance, and the actual MySQL database that will be used by the application will be called the database (shown as **DB** in the diagram).

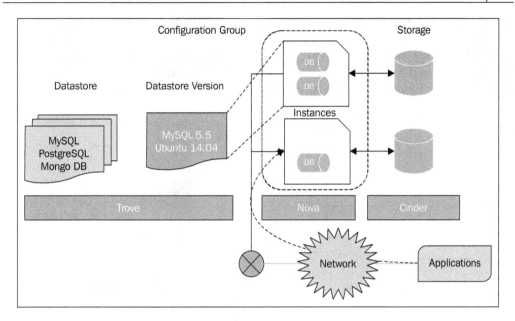

A multi-datastore scenario

One of the important features of the Trove system is that it supports multiple databases to various degrees. In this subsection, we will see how Trove works with multiple Trove datastores.

In the following diagram, we have represented all the components of Trove (the API, task manager, and conductor) except the **Guest Agent** databases as **Trove Controller**. The **Guest Agent** code is different for every datastore that needs to be supported and the **Guest Agent** for that particular datastore is installed on the corresponding image of the datastore version.

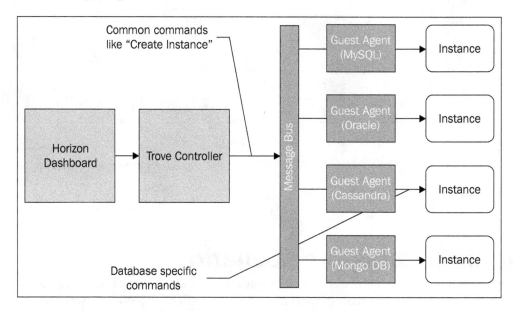

The guest agents by default have to implement some of the basic actions for the datastore, namely, create, resize, and delete, and individual guest agents have extensions that enable them to support additional features just for that datastore.

The following diagram should help us understand the command proxy function of the guest agent. Please note that the commands shown are only indicative, and the actual commands will vary.

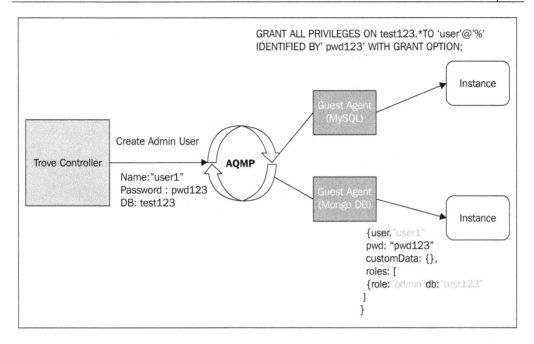

At the time of writing this book, Trove's guest agents are installable only on Linux; hence, only databases on Linux systems are supported. Feature requests (`https://blueprints.launchpad.net/trove/+spec/mssql-server-db-support`) were created for the ability to create a guest agent for Windows and support Microsoft SQL databases, but they have not yet been approved at the time of writing this and might be a remote possibility.

Database software distribution support

Trove supports various databases; the following table shows the databases supported by this service at the time of writing this. Automated installation is available for all the different databases, but there is some level of difference when it comes to the configuration capabilities of Trove with respect to different databases.

This has lot to do with the lack of a common configuration base among the different databases. At the time of writing this book, MySQL and MariaDB have the most configuration options available, as shown in this list:

Database	Version
MySQL	5.5, 5.6
Percona	5.5, 5.6
MariaDB	5.5, 10.0
Couchbase	2.2, 3.0
Cassandra	2.1
Redis	2.8
PostgreSQL	9.3, 9.4
MongoDB	2.6, 3.0
DB2 Expre	10.5
CouchDB	1.6

So, as you can see, almost all the major database applications that can run on Linux are already supported on Trove.

Putting it all together

Now that you have understood the architecture and terminologies, we will take a look at the general steps that are followed:

1. Horizon/Trove CLI requests a new database instance and passes the datastore name and version, along with the flavor ID and volume size as mandatory parameters. Optional parameters such as the configuration group, AZ, replica-of, and so on can also be passed.

2. The Trove API requests Nova for an instance with the particular image and a Cinder volume of a specific size to be added to the instance.

3. The Nova instance boots and follows these steps:

    1. The cloud-init scripts are run (like all other Nova instances).

    2. The configuration files (for example, `trove-guestagent.conf`) are copied down to the instance.

    3. The guest agent is installed.

4. The Trove API will also have sent the request to the task manager, which will then send the `prepare` call to the message bus topic.

5. After booting, the guest agent listens to the message bus for any activities for it to do, and once it finds a message for itself, it processes the `prepare` command and performs the following functions:

   ° Installing the database distribution (if not already installed on the image)

   ° Creating the configuration file with the default configuration for the database engine (and any configuration from the configuration groups associated overriding the defaults)

   ° Starting the database engine and enabling auto-start

   ° Polling the database engine for availability (until the database engine is available or the timeout is reached)

   ° Reporting the status back to the Trove backend using the Trove conductor

6. The Trove manager reports back to the API and the status of the machine is changed.

Use cases

So, if you are wondering all the places where we can use Trove, it fits in rather nicely with the following use cases.

Dev/test databases

Dev/test databases are an absolute killer feature, and almost all companies that start using Trove will definitely use it for their dev/test environments. This provides developers with the ability to freely create and dispose of database instances at will. This ability helps them be more productive and removes any lag from when they want it to when they get it.

The capability of being able to take a backup, run a database, and restore the backup to another server is especially key when it comes to these kinds of workloads.

Web application databases

Trove is used in production for any database that supports low-risk applications, such as some web applications. With the introduction of different redundancy mechanisms, such as master-slave in MySQL, this is becoming more suited to many production environments.

Features

Trove is moving fast in terms of the features being added in the various releases. In this section, we will take a look at the features of three releases: the current release and the past two.

The Juno release

The Juno release saw a lot of features being added to the Trove system. Here is a non-exhaustive list:

- Support for Neutron: Now we can use both Nova-network and Neutron for networking purposes.
- Replication: MySQL master/slave replication was added. The API also allowed us to detach a slave for it to be promoted.
- Clustering: MongoDB cluster support was added.
- Configuration group improvements:

    ○ The functionality of using a default configuration group for a datastore version was added. This allows us to build the datastore version with a base configuration of your company standards.

    ○ Basic error checking was added to configuration groups.

The Kilo release

The Kilo release majorly worked on introducing a new datastore. The following is the list of major features that were introduced:

- Support for the **GTID** (short for **global transaction identifier**) replication strategy
- New datastores, namely Vertica, DB2, and CouchDB, are supported

The Liberty release

The Liberty release introduced the following features to Trove. This is a non-exhaustive list:

- Configuration groups for Redis and MongoDB
- Cluster support for Redis and MongoDB
- Percona XtraDB cluster support

- Backup and restore for a single instance of MongoDB
- User and database management for MongoDB
- Horizon support for database clusters
- A management API for datastores and versions
- The ability to deploy Trove instances in a single admin tenant so that the Nova instances are hidden from the user

In order to see all the features introduced in the releases, please look at the release notes of the system, which can be found at these URLs:

Juno : `https://wiki.openstack.org/wiki/ReleaseNotes/Juno`

Kilo : `https://wiki.openstack.org/wiki/ReleaseNotes/Kilo`

Liberty : `https://wiki.openstack.org/wiki/ReleaseNotes/Liberty`

Summary

In this chapter, we were introduced to the basic concepts of DBaaS and how Trove can help with this. With several changes being introduced and a score of one on five with respect to maturity, it might seem as if it is too early to adopt Trove. However, a lot of companies are giving Trove a go in their dev/test environments as well as for some web databases in production, which is why the adoption percentage is steadily on the rise.

A few companies that are using Trove today are giants such as eBay, who run their dev/test Test databases on Trove; HP Helion Cloud, Rackspace Cloud, and Tesora (which is also one of the biggest contributors to the project) have DBaaS offerings based on the Trove component.

Trove is increasingly being used in various companies, and it is helping in reducing DBAs' mundane work and improving standardization. In the next chapter, we will see how to quickly set up Trove using DevStack scripts.

2
Setting up Trove with DevStack in a Box

There are several distributions of OpenStack that are available out there and almost all of them can be used along with Trove. Since the focus of this book is Trove and not so much deploying OpenStack itself, we will set up Trove along with DevStack, which is a script that helps in quickly setting up a development environment of OpenStack.

In this chapter, we will look at setting up our Stack in a single node deployment and follow up with setting up the Trove system. In brief, this chapter will deal with:

- Prerequisites for following along with this book
- Understanding DevStack and its components
- Setting up the Trove system with DevStack
- Working with screen and performing some functions in DevStack

At the end of the book, we will have a working Trove install in less than a couple of hours. It is not recommended to use this method (using DevStack) to roll out a production environment.

Requirements

In order to use DevStack, the requirements are fairly minimal and the setup is fairly easy. We can set up a range of deployments right from a single node deployment to a multiple node deployment in a few moments. The following list shows what we need.

Operating system

DevStack runs on Ubuntu, RHEL, and Fedora and can work on most other popular Linux distributions. The latest releases of these operating systems are supported. In this book, we will be using Ubuntu 14.04 as our base operating system for the DevStack install.

Database

From a database perspective, DevStack runs with MySQL (or Maria DB) and PostgreSQL. We will be using Maria DB (the open source fork of MySQL) in this book.

Messaging queue

DevStack supports both RabbitMQ and QPID. In this book, we will be using RabbitMQ.

Web server

Apache is supported by DevStack and we will be using this in our installation.

Internet connection

Internet connection is a must as the script will pull the actual repositories from GitHub in order to install the OpenStack services. You can use a direct Internet connection or a connection through a proxy.

 The process to use a proxy is shown in the following sections, but please note that this is completely optional and only to be used when we are using a proxy in an enterprise lab environment. If not using the proxy, you can safely ignore these commands.

Preparing the server

We will be creating a single node install of DevStack and be using Nova networking, rather than Neutron networking for the sake of simplicity.

It is possible to run DevStack in multiple environments, right from running it on a **virtual machine** (**VM**) in your laptop/desktop, physical hardware, or even in public cloud environments like Azure and Rackspace.

In this book, we will create our VM running on an ESXi server in our lab environment. The only limitation in following this approach is that we will be able to use only QEMU as opposed to KVM (we can edit to pass the 64 bit flags up, but that will not give us true 64 bit in the nested hypervisor environment).

Minimum configuration required

In order to run DevStack, the following are the bare minimum requirements:

- RAM: 4 GB
- CPU: 2 cores
- Disk: 20 GB
- Internet connection: Yes
- Operating system: DevStack-supported operating system

We will be using this environment later to show replication, backup, and so on. For running some serious tests, we may need at least twice or thrice the amount of processing power and memory mentioned in the preceding list.

Server configuration

The server configuration that we are using is as follows:

- RAM: 8 GB
- CPU: 4 cores
- Hard disk 1: 40 GB
- Hard disk 2: 40 GB
- Operating system: Ubuntu 14.04
- NIC card: 1
- Internet connection: via HTTP proxy
- Proxy authentication needed: No

The proxy is being used deliberately in this book, so as to show how to install DevStack with a proxy in play. The second hard drive can be added later for the Cinder service to create its volumes on.

Setting the IP address

We will set a static IP address onto our server. We will need the following information. Please fill in the table with the relevant information as applicable to your environment:

Name	Value
IP address	172.22.6.246
Default gateway	172.22.6.1
Subnet mask	255.255.255.0
DNS server	172.22.6.35

We will edit the file /etc/network/interfaces and set eth0 (or the appropriate interface) with the static IP address. The eth0 section will look something like this:

```
iface eth0 inet static
address 172.22.6.246
gateway 172.22.6.1
netmask 255.255.255.0
dns-nameservers 172.22.6.35
```

The first line specifies that the interface eth0 will have an inet (IPv4) address and is static. The remaining lines are self-explanatory.

After this, please restart the service using the command:

```
service networking restart
```

If you have a desktop install, or are using the network configuration manager to set the IP address, you will have to first disable it by editing the file at /etc/NetworkManager/NetworkManager.conf and disabling the DNS masquerading and setting the managed under the [ifupdown] section to true.

Once the configuration is set, please type the ifconfig command to verify:

```
ifconfig -a
```

```
alokas@DevStack:~$ ifconfig -a
eth0      Link encap:Ethernet  HWaddr 00:50:56:97:74:75
          inet addr:172.22.6.246  Bcast:172.22.6.255  Mask:255.255.255.0
          inet6 addr: fe80::250:56ff:fe97:7475/64 Scope:Link
          inet6 addr: fc00:172:22:6:250:56ff:fe97:7475/64 Scope:Global
          inet6 addr: fc00:172:22:6:d9ba:f621:217:75d0/64 Scope:Global
          UP BROADCAST RUNNING MULTICAST  MTU:1500  Metric:1
          RX packets:3230 errors:0 dropped:0 overruns:0 frame:0
          TX packets:89 errors:0 dropped:0 overruns:0 carrier:0
          collisions:0 txqueuelen:1000
          RX bytes:229525 (229.5 KB)  TX bytes:12975 (12.9 KB)

lo        Link encap:Local Loopback
          inet addr:127.0.0.1  Mask:255.0.0.0
          inet6 addr: ::1/128 Scope:Host
          UP LOOPBACK RUNNING  MTU:65536  Metric:1
          RX packets:32 errors:0 dropped:0 overruns:0 frame:0
          TX packets:32 errors:0 dropped:0 overruns:0 carrier:0
          collisions:0 txqueuelen:0
          RX bytes:2368 (2.3 KB)  TX bytes:2368 (2.3 KB)
```

Please verify that the IP address was assigned. You can check the default gateway by typing the command:

```
netstat -rn
```

You should also verify that the DNS servers were set in the file /etc/resolv.conf, by using the command:

```
cat /etc/resolv.conf
```

Installing prerequisites

Before we can run the DevStack script, we will have to perform a couple of prerequisite actions:

- Add a user and give it sudoers access
- Install packages

Adding a user

We will create a user called stack and give that user sudoers permission. We will need root access to do so.

```
sudo su
```

```
adduser stack
```

This will create the user and also creates the home directory for the user. We will now give this user all sudoers permissions as this user will be the one to install all the different components. When a list of questions appears, just select all the defaults.

```
echo "stack ALL=(ALL) NOPASSWD: ALL" | sudo tee -a /etc/sudoers
```

Executing this command will add the user stack to the sudoers file allowing the stack user with all the permissions. We could even put the stack user in the admin group, but then it will need a password, hence this method is followed.

Installing packages

There are a few packages we will need to install before we can proceed any further:

- git: This package provides the git command line to clone the repositories.
- screen: This provides a screen where we can execute long running commands without being interrupted. This is needed so that the installation can continue even if we accidently close the session.
- corkscrew: This is used if we need to tunnel the git using the HTTP proxy (as we will be doing in our case).

The following command will install these packages:

```
sudo apt-get clean
sudo apt-get update
sudo apt-get install git screen corkscrew
```

Once the installation is complete, we can proceed to actual installation of DevStack itself.

DevStack

DevStack, as we have already discussed, is a script that installs the other OpenStack components in a development environment. There are several modes in which DevStack can be installed, but the only thoroughly tested mode is the All-In-One Single box installation.

The DevStack script itself is located on the GitHub and needs to be pulled from there. This ensures that we always have the latest script.

Downloading the DevStack script

DevStack can be downloaded by the `git clone` command. We will clone that in our home directory.

```
cd ~
git clone https://git.openstack.org/openstack-dev/devstack
```

This will clone the DevStack project onto the local `devstack` folder. Since we are using a proxy server, this may not work right off the bat. If you don't have a proxy server, then you can skip this section.

Using a proxy with GitHub

In order to make `git` work with a proxy, we will use corkscrew. We will need the following information:

Name	Value
Proxy IP	172.21.2.17
Proxy port	80
Proxy username	NA
Proxy password	NA

In order to perform a read-only operation, we will need to create a file in some location; in our case, we will create a file, `mygitproxy.sh`, in our home directory.

We will need to add the following lines to the file and set it in the proxy configuration of `git`:

```
#!/bin/bash
exec corkscrew <Proxy IP> <Proxy Port> $*
```

In our case, we will create the file and substitute our proxy IP and proxy port. Copying and pasting the following will create the file called `mygitproxy.sh` and the contents of the file are delimited using the EOT:

```
cat <<EOT >> /home/alokas/mygitproxy.sh
#!/bin/bash
exec corkscrew 172.21.2.17 80 \$*
EOT
```

We also have to change the permission for this file to be executable by using the chmod command.

```
chmod +x /home/alokas/mygitproxy.sh
```

The contents of the file are as shown in the following screenshot:

```
alokas@DevStack:~$ cat mygitproxy.sh
#!/bin/bash

exec corkscrew 172.21.2.17 80 $*
alokas@DevStack:~$
alokas@DevStack:~$ chmod +x /home/alokas/mygitproxy.sh
```

As a last step, we have to now change the git global configuration to use this file, which is done by using the following command:

```
git config --global core.gitproxy '/home/alokas/mygitproxy.sh'
```

We also have to set the environment variables: http_proxy, https_proxy and no_proxy.

```
export http_proxy=http://172.21.2.17:80
```

```
export https_proxy=http://172.21.2.17:80
```

```
export no_proxy=localhost,172.22.6.0/24
```

The http and https_proxy commands set the proxies to be used and no_proxy is used to ignore the proxy. We will need to provide the details of our local networks, so that the local connections are not proxied.

 We know that the different components in the OpenStack system talk to each other by using the HTTP RESTful API calls. The purpose of setting no_proxy is simply to ensure that those calls don't go through the proxy and fail.

We should now be able to execute the git clone command that was mentioned in the earlier section (cd ~ && git clone https://git.openstack.org/openstack-dev/devstack).

```
alokas@DevStack:~$ git clone https://git.openstack.org/openstack-dev/devstack
Cloning into 'devstack'...
remote: Counting objects: 29786, done.
remote: Compressing objects: 100% (14000/14000), done.
remote: Total 29786 (delta 21203), reused 23688 (delta 15452)
Receiving objects: 100% (29786/29786), 5.91 MiB | 224.00 KiB/s, done.
Resolving deltas: 100% (21203/21203), done.
Checking connectivity... done.
```

The devstack repository is now cloned onto your local environment. Please change to that directory by typing the command:

cd ~/devstack

We are now in the DevStack directory, which we have just cloned from git.

Understanding the DevStack files

Once in the directory, you will see several files and scripts. Although it is not necessary to know what these scripts do in detail, it is definitely a good idea to know the contents.

stack.sh

Being the most important script in the directory, stack.sh is used to install the different components of OpenStack. This script allows us to specify configuration options of which git repositories to use, what are the services you want to be enabled in your environment, and their network configurations and so on. It uses a configuration file called stackrc for this purpose, which has most of the user configuration information.

unstack.sh

As the name suggests, unstack.sh is used to stop all OpenStack services except common services like MySQL and RabbitMQ.

rejoin-stack.sh

The rejoin-stack.sh script rejoins an existing screen, or re-creates a screen session from a previous run of stack.sh. This is used after you have rebooted the server and would want to go back to where you left off. We will need to run this script and the VMs that we created and the data will be restored.

Please be advised that the rejoin stack doesn't actually power on the guest VMs running on OpenStack. You have to manually power them up from the Horizon dashboard or the CLI commands.

run_test.sh

The `run_test.sh` script runs tests on the entire project for any stray white spaces and major style formatting. We would use this if we were contributing to the DevStack code itself; however, in this book, we won't have much use for this script.

exercise.sh

The function of this script is to run all the examples present in the `devstack/exercises` directory and report on the results. The directory already has some scripts to demonstrate the capabilities of OpenStack; we may choose to add some more files in the directory.

clean.sh

The function of this script is to remove all the files used by OpenStack. In case you run this, you may need to download all the files again.

local.sh

The function of this script (found in the samples directory) is to run some additional scripts after `stack.sh` has completed its job. We need to copy this to the base directory for it to function properly.

Configuring the DevStack installation

DevStack uses the `stackrc` file located in the base directory. However, the settings of `stackrc` can be overridden by the `local.conf` file if placed in the root directory. A copy of the `local.conf` file can be found in the samples directory.

By default, the following services will be installed when running DevStack:

- Nova (API, Certificate, Object Store, Compute, Network, Scheduler, VNC proxies, Certificate Authentication): Compute service
- Cinder (Scheduler, API, Volume): Block volumes
- Glance (API and Registry): Image store

- Horizon: Dashboard
- Keystone: Identity
- MySQL: Database
- RabbitMQ: Message bus
- Tempest: OpenStack Integration Test Suite

We can also install other components like Swift, Heat, Ceilometer, Trove, and so on by modifying the `stackrc` file or the `localrc` file.

Although Tempest is going to be installed, we will not be using it in this book as we are not going to be developing anything in OpenStack itself.

Before we start configuring the `local.conf` file in order to provide the install and configure options to the `stack.sh` script, here are a few things that we need to keep handy for us to modify:

Name	Name in config file	Value
Password for MySQL root user	DATABASE_PASSWORD	dbr00tpwd
Password for RabbitMQ	RABBIT_PASSWORD	rabb1tpwd
Passwords for different OpenStack service accounts	SERVICE_PASSWORD	oss3rvice
Password for admin account	ADMIN_PASSWORD	adm1npwd
Random service token	SERVICE_TOKEN	x1y1z1token
IP range for instances	FIXED_RANGE	10.1.10.0/24
Floating IP range	FLOATING_RANGE	192.168.1.0/27
Interface	FLAT_INTERFACE	eth0
Number of IPs in the range for instances	FIXED_NETWORK_SIZE	256

This is all the information we need to get started. Please note that in this case, we are using Nova networking and a simple flat network, where all the instances will be connected to the same bridge and can talk to each other.

If we do decide to use Neutron networking, then some additional settings need to be added.

The `localrc` settings need to look like the following:

```
FLOATING_RANGE=192.168.1.0/27
FIXED_RANGE=10.1.10.0/24
FIXED_NETWORK_SIZE=256
FLAT_INTERFACE=eth0
ADMIN_PASSWORD=adm1npwd
DATABASE_PASSWORD=dbr00tpwd
RABBIT_PASSWORD=rabb1tpwd
SERVICE_PASSWORD=oss3rvice
SERVICE_TOKEN=x1y1z1token
```

Please ensure there are no spaces between the equal sign and the values themselves, otherwise the script will fail midway.

Step 1 – copy the local.conf file from the samples directory to the base directory

Assuming that you have also cloned `devstack` in your home directory, let us change the directory.

```
cd ~/devstack
cp samples/local.conf ./
```

```
alokas@DevStack:/var$ cd ~/devstack
alokas@DevStack:~/devstack$ cp samples/local.conf ./
alokas@DevStack:~/devstack$ ls
clean.sh        exercises       functions-common  lib                openrc            samples      tests
doc             exercise.sh     FUTURE.rst        LICENSE            pkg               setup.cfg    tools
driver_certs    extras.d        gate              local.conf         README.md         setup.py     tox.ini
eucarc          files           HACKING.rst       MAINTAINERS.rst    rejoin-stack.sh   stackrc      unstack.sh
exerciserc      functions       inc               Makefile           run_tests.sh      stack.sh
alokas@DevStack:~/devstack$
```

You should see the `local.conf` file copied to the base directory. This will be the only file we need to edit in order to install.

Step 2 – modify the localrc section

Under the `[[local|localrc]]` section, we have to modify the settings with the values that we have just defined. After the edit, the file will look like the following screenshot:

```
alokas@DevStack:~/devstack$ vim local.conf
alokas@DevStack:~/devstack$ cat local.conf | egrep -v "#" | egrep -v "^$"
[[local|localrc]]
FLOATING_RANGE=192.168.1.0/27
FIXED_RANGE=10.1.10.0/24
FIXED_NETWORK_SIZE=256
FLAT_INTERFACE=eth0
ADMIN_PASSWORD=adm1npwd
DATABASE_PASSWORD= dbr00tpwd
RABBIT_PASSWORD=rabb1tpwd
SERVICE_PASSWORD=oss3rvice
SERVICE_TOKEN=x1y1z1token
LOGFILE=$DEST/logs/stack.sh.log
LOGDAYS=2
SWIFT_HASH=66a3d6b56c1f479c8b4e70ab5c2000f5
SWIFT_REPLICAS=1
SWIFT_DATA_DIR=$DEST/data
enable_service tempest
alokas@DevStack:~/devstack$
```

Step 3 – modify the local.conf to install Trove and Swift

As a final step, we will enable Trove and Swift (for database backups).
The following commands will append the lines between the delimiters (EOF)
to the `local.conf` file.

Before executing the command, let us take a look at how this all works.
`ENABLED_SERVICES` is an array, which is used by the `stack.sh` script to install
and configure the different OpenStack services. `+=` appends to the array and
`-=` takes away from the array.

So essentially, we enable the Swift and Trove services. We also enable the installation
of the Trove client by enabling the plugin:

```
cd ~/devstack
```

```
cat <<EOF  >> local.conf
```

```
ENABLED_SERVICES+=,trove,tr-api,tr-tmgr,tr-cond
```

```
enable_plugin trove git://git.openstack.org/openstack/trove
```

```
enable_plugin python-troveclient git://git.openstack.org/openstack/
python-troveclient
```

```
ENABLED_SERVICES+=,s-proxy,s-object,s-container,s-account
```

```
EOF
```

Enabling Neutron

Optionally, we can enable Neutron networking by adding the following lines to the `local.conf`:

`ENABLED_SERVICES +=,neutron,q-meta,q-l3,q-dhcp,q-agt,q-svc`

`ENABLED_SERVICES -= n-net`

This simply enables the Neutron services and disables the Nova networking service. But, for the sake of simplicity, we will not be using Neutron in this book.

That's it, we are now ready to install DevStack in our environment.

Installing DevStack

DevStack is normally installed with a single command. However, this takes a very long time to complete and, in order to save ourselves the trouble of being disconnected from the SSH session and having to restart the entire install, we will use screen.

Screen is a program that helps to open several terminal instances on one single physical terminal instance.

We will start a screen session and run the installer (typing the `screen` command starts a new screen session).

```
screen
cd ~/devstack
./stack.sh
```

You can then either monitor the progress or disconnect from the screen (by pressing *Ctrl + A* and *Ctrl + D*) and let the process run on the backend. When you want to go back to the screen, please type `screen -r` (to reconnect).

Running the `stack.sh` script will run several things and will install the OpenStack components that have been selected in the `stackrc` file. However, since we are using a proxy server, we have to make some simple additional changes before we can run with it.

Using a proxy server

Please follow this section only while using a proxy server to install DevStack, otherwise, skip it completely.

We need to make the following changes:

- Export the proxy variables
- Add GIT_BASE to the local section of the local.conf file

We can export the proxy variables as we did in the previous section when we were cloning DevStack itself.

```
export http_proxy=http://172.21.2.17:80
```

```
export https_proxy=http://172.21.2.17:80
```

```
export no_proxy=localhost,172.22.6.0/24
```

Using your favorite editor, go ahead and edit the local.conf file (as we did in the previous section); add a line as shown:

```
GIT_BASE=http://github.com
```

The local.conf file will have the contents as shown in the following screen capture:

```
alokas@DevStack:~/devstack$ cat local.conf | egrep -v "#" | egrep -v "^$"
[[local|localrc]]
GIT_BASE=http://github.com
FLOATING_RANGE=192.168.1.0/27
FIXED_RANGE=10.1.10.0/24
FIXED_NETWORK_SIZE=256
FLAT_INTERFACE=eth0
ADMIN_PASSWORD=adm1npwd
DATABASE_PASSWORD=dbr00tpwd
RABBIT_PASSWORD=rabb1tpwd
SERVICE_PASSWORD=oss3rvice
SERVICE_TOKEN=x1y1z1token
LOGFILE=$DEST/logs/stack.sh.log
LOGDAYS=2
SWIFT_HASH=66a3d6b56c1f479c8b4e70ab5c2000f5
SWIFT_REPLICAS=1
SWIFT_DATA_DIR=$DEST/data
enable_service tempest
alokas@DevStack:~/devstack$
```

Once this is complete, we can now just run the stack.sh script, which will spew out a ton of output of the actions it is performing. Once that is complete, the script will give you the URLs to access your new OpenStack deployment.

Please use the same three commands mentioned to start the installation.

```
screen
```

```
cd ~/devstack
```

```
./stack.sh
```

The script will start the installation as shown in the following screen capture:

```
alokas@DevStack:~/devstack$ ./stack.sh
+ unset GREP_OPTIONS
+ umask 022
+ PATH=/usr/local/sbin:/usr/local/bin:/usr/sbin:/usr/bin:/sbin:/bin:/usr/games
sr/sbin:/sbin
+++ dirname ./stack.sh
++ cd .
++ pwd
+ TOP_DIR=/home/alokas/devstack
+ NOUNSET=
+ [[ -n '' ]]
+ [[ -r /home/alokas/devstack/.stackenv ]]
+ FILES=/home/alokas/devstack/files
+ '[' '!' -d /home/alokas/devstack/files ']'
+ '[' '!' -d /home/alokas/devstack/inc ']'
+ '[' '!' -d /home/alokas/devstack/lib ']'
+ [[ '' == \y ]]
+ [[ 1000 -eq 0 ]]
+ [[ -e /home/alokas/.no-devstack ]]
+ LAST_SPINNER_PID=
+ source /home/alokas/devstack/functions
++ [[ -z '' ]]
```

During the process of the installation, it may ask you for your password for the sudoers access and any other passwords that you may not have specified in the local.conf file.

After this, depending on your Internet connection speed, you may have to wait for several minutes or hours for the packages to be downloaded and installed on your server.

The DevStack script clones all the different OpenStack components in the /opt/stack folder. You can navigate to this folder and see what individual services are cloned in the individual folders under this base folder.

We will need to reconnect to the screen session to see the output if we have disconnected, by typing:

```
screen -r
```

During the installation, you will also see that there are additional screens that are started as the DevStack script (this screen is called stack).

```
alokas@DevStack:~$ screen -r
There are several suitable screens on:
        7309.stack          (10/13/2015 07:08:58 AM)            (Detached)
        2237.pts-0.DevStack      (10/13/2015 07:02:07 AM)             (Detached)
Type "screen [-d] -r [pid.]tty.host" to resume one of them.
```

In this case, we know that our screen is the one that is not stack, so we will connect to it by passing PID.TTY.Host in the command as shown:

```
screen -r 2237.pts-0.DevStack
```

Once the installation is complete, the script will give an output in the following format:

```
This is your host IP address: 172.22.6.246
This is your host IPv6 address: fc00:172:22:6:250:56ff:fe97:7475
Horizon is now available at http://172.22.6.246/dashboard
Keystone is serving at http://172.22.6.246:5000/
The default users are: admin and demo
The password: adm1npwd
```

Our stack in the box is ready. It should have installed Horizon, Nova, Keystone, Cinder, Trove, and Swift. We can now log in to the Horizon portal with the URL mentioned.

Verifying the installation

If we don't have any errors in the log file, the stack should be ready. However, let's complete a few quick verification tasks before we go to the next section.

The first thing that we will do is log in to the horizon portal, the URL of which has been outputted by the `stack.sh` script. In our case, it is `http://172.22.6.246/dashboard`. We need to be able to log in with the credentials that we choose in the configuration file.

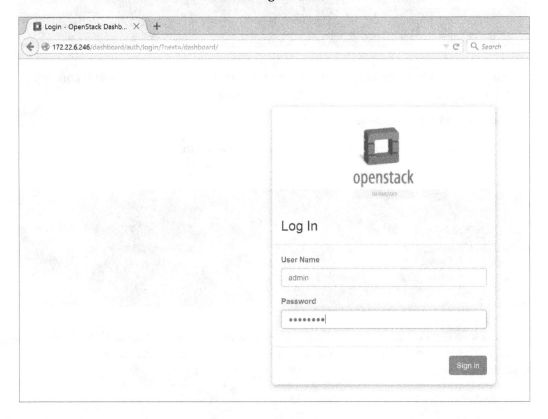

Once you are able to log in, navigate to **System | System Information**. This screen should be able to show you the status of the components of OpenStack that were installed.

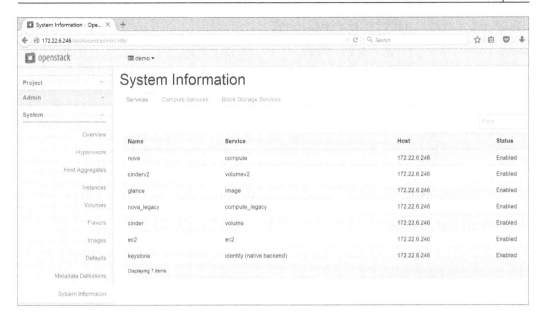

You should be able to see all the services that are installed and the hosts on which they are installed. Since this is a single node installation, all the services will be installed on the same server. However, if you have done a multi-node install, then we will be able to see multiple servers listed in the services.

Please feel free to navigate around the Horizon portal and explore it; you will see that there are two tenants that are created: admin tenant and demo tenant. The admin user will have access to both of the tenants.

Troubleshooting the install

If there have been issues with the install, please navigate to the /opt/stack/logs directory and look for stack.sh.log. This will show all the activities that the script performed, and will point out what caused the failure.

Working with screen

Since we are using DevStack in this book, screen becomes a core concept of running DevStack. In this section, we will take a look at some screen commands and how we will be using them in order to interact with DevStack.

Screen is software that essentially is a window manager in Linux. It helps the user to use multiple shell windows from a single SSH session. This is recommended to be used when we have a long running command that needs to survive network disruptions.

Screen is normally used to run long running processes. DevStack creates and runs its entire services in its own screen and if you were to use the `~/devstack/restack.sh` script, it would connect you to the already running screen session.

We installed screen as a prerequisite earlier in the chapter; let us now look at some of the commands that will help us.

Screen control key

Pressing *Ctrl + A* activates the control mode and any key you press after that is passed as a control key and not as a key press sent to the shell.

In order to use this, you have to press *Ctrl + A*, release, and press the key that you want to send as a command.

For example, for help, you would press *Ctrl + A*, release it, and then press the *?* key.

Useful commands

Some of the useful commands in screen are as follows:

* `screen <screen name>`: To create a new screen session
* `screen -ls`: To list all the screen sessions
* `screen -r <screen name>`: To reconnect to a screen
* `screen -X -S <screen name> <command>`: To pass a command to the screen

Once inside the screen, the following commands can come in handy:

* *Ctrl + A* and then *?*: Screen help page
* *Ctrl + A* and then *"* (Control key and double quotes): List of all windows in a screen (especially helpful to select the different services running in DevStack)

- *Ctrl + A* and then *C*: Create a window in screen
- *Ctrl + A* and then *N*: Go to next window
- *Ctrl + A* and then *D*: Detach from the screen
- *Ctrl + A* and then *K*: Kill the screen

DevStack and screen

Since DevStack runs in the screen called stack, we will be able to use all of the commands in order to manage the DevStack system. The screen windows keep debug logs of all the different services.

We should be able to find the screen name using the `screen -ls` command. The DevStack default screen name is **Stack**.

```
alokas@DevStack:~$ screen -ls
There is a screen on:
        20276.stack     (11/05/2015 07:56:06 PM)          (Detached)
1 Socket in /var/run/screen/S-alokas.
```

We could connect to it using the command `screen -r 20276.stack` (the name shown in the previous command output).

We can then see all the different services at a glance by using *Ctrl + A* and then ".

```
                                alokas@DevStack ~
Num Name

  0 shell
  1 dstat
  2 key
  3 key-access
  4 horizon
  5 s-proxy
  6 s-object
  7 s-container
  8 s-account
  9 g-reg
 10 g-api
 11 n-api
 12 n-cond
 13 n-crt
 14 n-net
 15 n-sch
 16 n-novnc
 17 n-cauth
 18 n-cpu
 19 c-api
 20 c-sch
 21 c-vol
 22 tr-api
 23 tr-tmgr
 24 tr-cond
```

We could switch to the window running a particular service by using the up and down arrows and hitting enter.

Killing DevStack

We could kill the stack by using the command:

```
screen -X -S 20276.stack quit
```

That sends the `quit` command to the screen thereby killing all the services.

Restarting DevStack services

DevStack installs the services and opens a screen for the services. Since the startup scripts are not installed (like in the case of the production install), in order to restart the services, we will need to use the following procedure:

1. Connect to the stack screen by:

   ```
   screen -r 20276.stack
   ```

```
                                    alokas@DevStack: ~                           - □ ×
2015-10-13 11:46:36.257 DEBUG oslo_concurrency.processutils [req-3e00b70c-5906-4
287-874e-936ca43d9791 None None] Running cmd (subprocess): sudo cinder-rootwrap
/etc/cinder/rootwrap.conf env LC_ALL=C vgs --noheadings --unit=g -o name,size,fr
ee,lv_count,uuid --separator : --nosuffix stack-volumes-lvmdriver-1 from (pid=10
192) execute /usr/local/lib/python2.7/dist-packages/oslo_concurrency/processutil
s.py:230
2015-10-13 11:46:36.305 DEBUG oslo_concurrency.processutils [req-3e00b70c-5906-4
287-874e-936ca43d9791 None None] CMD "sudo cinder-rootwrap /etc/cinder/rootwrap.
conf env LC_ALL=C vgs --noheadings --unit=g -o name,size,free,lv_count,uuid --se
parator : --nosuffix stack-volumes-lvmdriver-1" returned: 0 in 0.049s from (pid=
10192) execute /usr/local/lib/python2.7/dist-packages/oslo_concurrency/processut
ils.py:260
2015-10-13 11:46:36.306 DEBUG oslo_concurrency.processutils [req-3e00b70c-5906-4
287-874e-936ca43d9791 None None] Running cmd (subprocess): sudo cinder-rootwrap
/etc/cinder/rootwrap.conf env LC_ALL=C lvs --noheadings --unit=g -o vg_name,name
,size --nosuffix stack-volumes-lvmdriver-1 from (pid=10192) execute /usr/local/l
ib/python2.7/dist-packages/oslo_concurrency/processutils.py:230
2015-10-13 11:46:36.356 DEBUG oslo_concurrency.processutils [req-3e00b70c-5906-4
287-874e-936ca43d9791 None None] CMD "sudo cinder-rootwrap /etc/cinder/rootwrap.
conf env LC_ALL=C lvs --noheadings --unit=g -o vg_name,name,size --nosuffix stac
k-volumes-lvmdriver-1" returned: 0 in 0.050s from (pid=10192) execute /usr/local
/lib/python2.7/dist-packages/oslo_concurrency/processutils.py:260

-novnc   13$(L) n-cauth   14$(L) n-cpu   15$(L) c-api   16$(L) c-sch   17$(L) c-vol*
```

2. You will see a screen like the preceding one.

3. Browse to the service you want to restart by pressing *Ctrl* + *A* and *N* (for next screen) and *Ctrl* + *A* and *P*, for the previous screen, until you reach the service. Please read the service name at the lower left-hand corner.

4. We could also use the other methods of navigating the screens as mentioned previously. In this example, we will navigate to the Nova Scheduler Service.

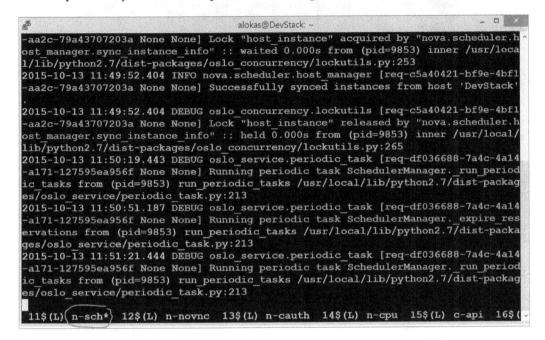

5. Press *Ctrl* + *C* to stop this service, and the prompt will return.

6. Press the up arrow (to see the last command) and press the *Enter* key to restart. This command is just a long command line with the location of the configuration file.

We could copy this command line and create our own startup scripts should we choose not to use this method.

```
                            alokas@DevStack: ~                        _ □ ×
lo_concurrency/lockutils.py:211
2015-10-13 11:52:19.448 DEBUG oslo_concurrency.lockutils [req-e772c26c-fa7d-4a06
-8915-47e8c53b7e39 None None] Acquired semaphore "singleton_lock" from (pid=9853
) lock /usr/local/lib/python2.7/dist-packages/oslo_concurrency/lockutils.py:198
2015-10-13 11:52:19.449 DEBUG oslo_concurrency.lockutils [req-e772c26c-fa7d-4a06
-8915-47e8c53b7e39 None None] Releasing semaphore "singleton_lock" from (pid=985
3) lock /usr/local/lib/python2.7/dist-packages/oslo_concurrency/lockutils.py:211
2015-10-13 11:52:19.450 INFO oslo_service.service [req-e772c26c-fa7d-4a06-8915-4
7e8c53b7e39 None None] Caught SIGINT, exiting
2015-10-13 11:52:19.450 WARNING oslo_messaging.server [req-e772c26c-fa7d-4a06-89
15-47e8c53b7e39 None None] start/stop/wait must be called in the same thread
2015-10-13 11:52:19.451 WARNING oslo_messaging.server [req-e772c26c-fa7d-4a06-89
15-47e8c53b7e39 None None] start/stop/wait must be called in the same thread
2015-10-13 11:52:22.412 DEBUG oslo_concurrency.lockutils [req-e772c26c-fa7d-4a06
-8915-47e8c53b7e39 None None] Acquired semaphore "singleton_lock" from (pid=9853
) lock /usr/local/lib/python2.7/dist-packages/oslo_concurrency/lockutils.py:198
2015-10-13 11:52:22.412 DEBUG oslo_concurrency.lockutils [req-e772c26c-fa7d-4a06
-8915-47e8c53b7e39 None None] Releasing semaphore "singleton_lock" from (pid=985
3) lock /usr/local/lib/python2.7/dist-packages/oslo_concurrency/lockutils.py:211
alokas@DevStack:~/devstack$
alokas@DevStack:~/devstack$ /usr/local/bin/nova-scheduler --config-file /etc/nov
a/nova.conf & echo $! >/opt/stack/status/stack/n-sch.pid; fg || echo "n-sch fail
ed to start" | tee "/opt/stack/status/stack/n-sch.failure"
 11$(L) n-sch*  12$(L) n-novnc  13$(L) n-cauth  14$(L) n-cpu  15$(L) c-api  16$(
```

The service has now been restarted and we can continue to work on the server. We can use the other features of the screen with DevStack.

Summary

In this chapter, we learned how to use DevStack to get a stack in the box with Trove going quickly and easily. We understood DevStack files and installed and configured DevStack. We have also learned to work with screens.

Please do remember that DevStack is not to be used in a production environment, but can definitely be used to develop code or learn OpenStack quickly.

In the next chapter, we will talk about installing Trove in an existing OpenStack installation in a production setup.

3

Installing Trove in an Existing OpenStack Environment

In the previous chapter, we installed OpenStack with Trove on a single node using DevStack scripts. In this chapter, we will discuss how to add Trove onto your existing OpenStack installation.

Depending on the original distribution that was used to install OpenStack, the process for Trove will vary slightly and in all likelihood, we will use the same processes that we used for the other OpenStack components.

In this chapter, we will look at:

- Different deployment methods available for OpenStack
- Installing Trove from source
- Installing Trove from the Ubuntu repository

The installation itself is the simplest part of the process. Configuration is what takes most time and effort in the entire process. However, the good news is that the configuration is fairly similar for all the different distributions.

 You can skip this chapter for now and come back to it at a later point in time if the objective is to simply get started in Trove using the DevStack install, which we have done in the previous chapter. This chapter deals with getting this up and ready in a production environment so that on completion of this book, you may put the knowledge to use in a production environment.

Different methods of deploying OpenStack

Before we start adding Trove in our production environments, let's take a look at various methods that are available to install/deploy the OpenStack environment.

One method that we have already seen in the last chapter is utilizing DevStack scripts, but we also know that it is not fit for a production environment. There are several distributions of OpenStack, which can be downloaded from their repositories.

The most famous distributions for different categories are as follows:

- OS distribution: Ubuntu

    ° Installed using aptitude (apt-get) found on Debian systems and provides a repository for each release of OpenStack.

- Third-party distribution: Mirantis

    ° Installed and configured using another big-tent project called Fuel. The Trove plugin is available for us to use Fuel to install Trove.

- Distribution optimized for Trove: Tesora

    ° The distribution is available only as a DBaaS platform, which means if you have installed this, then you already have Trove.

There are other distributions like, say, **VIO** (short for **VMware Integrated OpenStack**), which has its own custom scripts to deploy OpenStack. In order to see which method users prefer, let's take a look at the user survey taken of OpenStack users about the different tools that are used to deploy OpenStack across various environments.

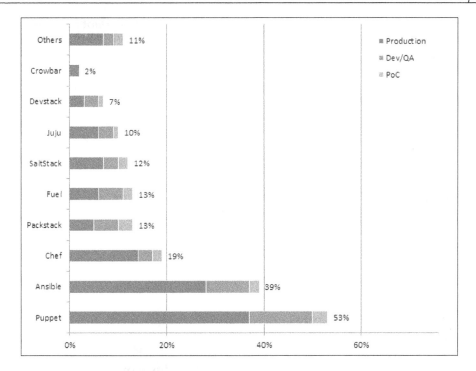

How to install Trove using all of the preceding tools will be exhaustive, time consuming, and will also need us to discuss the nature of the tools, which would fall outside the scope of this book. However, the scripts for some of them are listed next, which you can use for your production install:

- **SaltStack**: `https://github.com/saurabhsurana/trove-installer/tree/master/saltstack`

- **SaltStack-based OpenStack**: `https://github.com/EntropyWorks/salt-openstack`

- **OpenStack with Puppet**: `https://wiki.openstack.org/wiki/Puppet/Deploy`

- **OpenStack with Chef**: `https://docs.chef.io/openstack.html`

- **OpenStack with Ansible**: `https://github.com/openstack/openstack-ansible`

- **OpenStack with PackStack**: `https://wiki.openstack.org/wiki/Packstack`

- **OpenStack with Juju**: `https://jujucharms.com/openstack`

- **OpenStack with Fuel**: `https://wiki.openstack.org/wiki/Fuel`

Depending on what distribution you are using, they may or may not support Trove (most of them do) and in the event your distribution doesn't support Trove natively, you can install Trove from source as shown later in the chapter.

If your distribution supports Trove, then you would install it as you would install other OpenStack services. As an example, if you are using the Mirantis distro, then you would use Fuel and a Trove plugin to install Trove on your system.

Required OpenStack services

The best aspect of OpenStack is that you can choose to run services as per your requirement. However, there are some basic services that Trove and its features are dependent on; they need to be present:

- Keystone – for authentication
- Cinder – for block devices
- Swift – for backups
- Nova – for the VMs that would run the instances
- Horizon – for the GUI

Neutron is an optional component, and in its absence, the Nova network can provide the basic networking capabilities that are needed.

Keystone, Cinder, and Nova are mandatory, without which the service can't even perform its basic function. In the absence of Swift, the system will provide databases, but the backup/restore and replication/clusters and so on wouldn't work.

Planning the install

Before we go ahead with adding Trove to our production install, there are a couple of things we should do:

- Decide where to install the Trove components
- Take backups

Where to install the Trove components

In a production install of OpenStack, you would have a variety of nodes that would be functioning as:

- Controller node
- Compute node

- Storage node
- Network node

There might be a single node for each of these roles or multiples of these nodes depending on how large a footprint OpenStack is managing.

The best place you would install the services of Trove would be on the controller node, except of course the guest agent, which will be installed on the instance that Nova spins up.

If there are multiple controller nodes (in the case of an HA install of OpenStack), you will have to install the Trove components on both of them.

Take a backup

Now that we have chosen to use the controller node as the place where we will install the Trove server components, frequently, the controller node is normally virtual. It is a good idea to take a snapshot of the node, so if anything goes wrong, we will be able to restore it back to the current stage. If you are using a physical machine as the controller node, then this might not be easy, but you may still be able to take a snapshot using additional tools such as Acronis in order to take a physical snapshot.

Please note that this is an optional step and you may proceed without performing this.

Once the backup is complete, we can move on to installing the system and configuring it.

Installing Trove

We will take a look at installing Trove from its source and also using the Ubuntu OpenStack distribution repository.

Installing Trove from source

If our current distribution doesn't support Trove, or we have installed the production environment from source, we will have to choose to install Trove directly from source.

It is assumed that all the services that Trove requires (like Nova, Swift, and Keystone) are already installed and we also have the details about the supporting components like the MySQL and RabbitMQ services.

We will need to ensure that the following packages are installed. We just use aptitude to check and install them if they don't already exist.

```
sudo apt-get install build-essential libxslt1-dev qemu-utils mysql-client
sudo apt-get install python-dev python-pexpect python-mysqldb
libmysqlclient-dev
```

After this is complete, we will have to install the latest versions of setuptools and pip. We will install this in the user directory so as to not conflict with the system settings.

First, visit `https://pypi.python.org/pypi/setuptools/` and `https://pypi.python.org/pypi/pip/` to find out the latest version numbers.

We execute the following command to find the title of the pages that will give us the version number:

```
curl --silent https://pypi.python.org/pypi/setuptools/ | grep "<title>"
curl --silent https://pypi.python.org/pypi/pip/ | grep "<title>"
```

```
alokas@DevStack:~$ curl --silent https://pypi.python.org/pypi/setuptools/ | grep "<title>"
        <title>setuptools 18.4 : Python Package Index</title>
alokas@DevStack:~$ curl --silent https://pypi.python.org/pypi/pip/ | grep "<title>"
        <title>pip 7.1.2 : Python Package Index</title>
alokas@DevStack:~$
```

In our case, setuptools was at version 18.4 and the pip version was 7.1.2 as shown.

We will export these as variables.

```
export mypip=7.1.2
export myst=18.4
```

We will then download and install these in our home directory.

```
cd ~
wget https://pypi.python.org/packages/source/s/setuptools/setuptools-$myst.tar.gz
tar -xfvz setuptools-$myst.tar.gz
cd setuptools-$myst
python setup.py install -user
```

The preceding commands simply download the file, after substituting the version number, and unpack. That is, they will execute the install script as the user and not in the global realm. We will follow the same commands for pip as well.

```
wget https://pypi.python.org/packages/source/p/pip/pip-{{latest}}.tar.gz
tar xfvz pip-$mypip.tar.gz
cd pip-$mypip
python setup.py install -user
```

Once this completes, we will export our home directory as all the packages are installed in our home directory itself. We do this by sourcing the profile file.

```
echo PATH="$HOME/.local/bin:$PATH" >> ~/.profile
. ~/.profile
```

Since we don't want the main Python libraries to be touched, we will create a virtual environment and install Trove there. If you log out after you have created the virtual environment, just use the last line (`source env/bin/activate`) to get back to the virtual environment.

> We can ignore the creation/activation of the virtual environments (virtual environment and source commands to follow) if we don't mind the system libraries getting touched. This will happen in the case of production systems, as they will technically be installed to serve a single purpose, in this case running OpenStack.

In the virtual environment, we will clone the `git` repositories for Trove and its client.

```
pip install virtualenv --user
virtualenv --system-site-packages env
source env/bin/activate
cd ~
git clone https://git.openstack.org/openstack/trove.git
git clone https://git.openstack.org/openstack/python-troveclient.git
```

The preceding commands effectively clone the repositories onto the current directory, and Python is running in a virtual environment.

After this, we will quickly test the requirements and install Trove and its client.

```
cd ~/trove
pip install -r requirements.txt -r test-requirements.txt
sudo python setup.py install
cd ~/python-troveclient
sudo python setup.py install
```

 If you will also be developing the Trove system (which will not be the case in a production install), we can use the `sudo python setup.py` develop (replace the install with develop in the preceding two statements).

This will install Trove and its client. However, at this point in time, Trove is non-functional, and the configuration needs to be updated for this to function. The configuration process is the same as that of a production or multi-node deployment configuration. Therefore, please refer to the configuration section of the next installation procedure (*Configuring Trove*).

Installing with the Ubuntu OpenStack repository

In the case where we have an OpenStack production or a pre-production environment installed with Ubuntu's OpenStack distribution (install guides for the Liberty release can be found at `http://docs.openstack.org/liberty/install-guide-ubuntu/`), we can use the following section to add Trove on top of that.

Even if we have used, say, Puppet or Chef to install the OpenStack environment, it would have used the Ubuntu/Red Hat distro depending on the operating system of the node, so if you have an Ubuntu system, then chances are we can use this to add the Trove system.

We can install Trove by using the aptitude package manager.

```
apt-get install python-trove python-troveclient trove-common trove-api \
trove-taskmanager
```

It is assumed that the repositories will be set because we have already installed other components of OpenStack. Once the installation is complete, we will now be configuring the Trove system.

Installing the packages should also create a user called trove. We will verify that it is indeed the case; if not, we can add the user manually.

```
awk -F":" '{ print $1 }' /etc/passwd | grep -x trove
```

If we get an output on the screen, then the user exists. If we don't get an output, we can add it by using the command:

```
useradd -m trove -s /bin/bash
```

As the next step, we will configure the Trove system.

Configuring Trove

Configuring the Trove system is the final piece of the puzzle. If you have used an automated system (like SaltStack or DevStack), the configuration should automatically be done, provided the configuration parameters were passed down to the scripts.

If we have installed from source or from a repository manually, then the configuration becomes a mandatory part.

Before we start the configuration, we will need the following information handy. Some of this information will be new, and some of it will already exist based on the other components that are already installed (MySQL IP and Port, RabbitMQ server configuration, and so on).

We always follow a practice to fill out the details in a tabular format so that we can easily access them.

Please note that the table is filled with details from our existing environment, but these will be different for your environment.

Requirement	Value
Hostname/IP of controller node	172.22.6.246
Database IP and port	localhost:3306
RabbitMQ server	localhost
RabbitMQ username	stackrabbit
RabbitMQ password	rabb1tpwd
MySQL root password	dbr00tpwd
Keystone admin username	admin
Keystone admin password	adm1npwd
Trove password	oss3rvice
Trove DB password	tr0v3db

Setting up the MySQL database

We can log in to the MySQL server using the command:

```
mysql -u root -p
```

We will then create the database and assign user permissions to it. We could also use the root account to access the database. However, in a production environment, it is recommended that we use service accounts rather than the root account.

```
create database trove;
grant all privileges on trove.* TO trove@'localhost' identified by
'tr0v3db';

grant all privileges on trove.* TO trove@'%' identified by 'tr0v3db';
```

 We need both the lines because some versions of the database ignore `localhost` from the wild char `%`.

Keystone configuration

We will have to create the Trove user, service, and endpoint in the Keystone system. In order to do this, we will first export the required environment variables.

```
export OS_TENANT_NAME=admin
export OS_AUTH_URL=http://172.22.6.246:5000/v2.0
export OS_USERNAME=admin
export OS_PASSWORD=adm1npwd
```

We will also save this in a file and source it to export the variables for us.

```
keystone user-create --name trove -pass oss3rvice
keystone user-role-add --user trove --tenant service --role admin
```

This will create the user and add it as an admin in the service tenant. We will then create a service and its endpoint.

```
keystone service-create --name trove --type database --description
"Trove: The OpenStack Database Service"
```

This command will output the unique ID of the service, which you should note down and substitute in the following command to create the endpoint for the service.

Although the command mentions the region name as regionOne, you will have to set that to the region name being used in your environment.

```
keystone endpoint-create
--service-id <Insert Service ID here> \
--publicurl http:// 172.22.6.246:8779/v1.0/%\(tenant_id\)s \
--internalurl http://172.22.6.246:8779/v1.0/%\(tenant_id\)s \
--adminurl http://172.22.6.246:8779/v1.0/%\(tenant_id\)s \
--region regionOne
```

The Keystone endpoints can be verified by the command keystone endpoint-list or openstack endpoint list.

The details can be seen by the command `openstack endpoint show trove`.

```
alokas@DevStack:/etc/trove$ openstack endpoint show trove
+--------------+-------------------------------------------------+
| Field        | Value                                           |
+--------------+-------------------------------------------------+
| adminurl     | http://172.22.6.246:8779/v1.0/$(tenant_id)s     |
| enabled      | True                                            |
| id           | 4cab49691f014b6ba25d1a7eacc38b8c                |
| internalurl  | http://172.22.6.246:8779/v1.0/$(tenant_id)s     |
| publicurl    | http://172.22.6.246:8779/v1.0/$(tenant_id)s     |
| region       | RegionOne                                       |
| service_id   | 01d09303121244a29a0934222696e71e                |
| service_name | trove                                           |
| service_type | database                                        |
+--------------+-------------------------------------------------+
```

Modifying the configuration files

We will need to modify the following configuration files for Trove to work:

- `/etc/trove/trove-conductor.conf`
- `/etc/trove/trove.conf`
- `/etc/trove/trove-taskmanager.conf`
- `/etc/trove/trove-guestagent.conf`

trove.conf

In the main Trove configuration file, which is located at `/etc/trove/trove.conf`, we will edit the configuration to ensure the following is present. Please substitute the values from your environment, wherever applicable.

```
[DEFAULT]
trove_api_workers = 2
use_syslog = False
debug = True
default_datastore = mysql
sql_connection = mysql://trove:tr0v3db@localhost/trove
rabbit_password = rabb1tpwd
rabbit_userid = openstack
[keystone_authtoken]
signing_dir = /var/cache/trove
cafile = /opt/stack/data/ca-bundle.pem
auth_uri = http://172.22.6.246:5000
project_domain_id = default
project_name = service
```

```
user_domain_id = default
password = oss3rvice
username = trove
auth_url = http:// 172.22.6.246:35357
auth_plugin = password
```

trove-taskmanager.conf and trove-conductor.conf

Both the /etc/trove/trove-conductor.conf and /etc/trove/trove-taskmanager.conf files should be updated to contain the following:

```
[DEFAULT]
use_syslog = False
debug = True
trove_auth_url = http://172.22.6.246:35357/v2.0
nova_proxy_admin_pass =
nova_proxy_admin_tenant_name = trove
nova_proxy_admin_user = radmin
taskmanager_manager = trove.taskmanager.manager.Manager
sql_connection = mysql://trove:tr0v3db@localhost/trove
rabbit_password = rabb1tpwd
rabbit_userid = openstack
```

trove-guestagent.conf

This file is different in the sense that this is used by the guest agent, which is installed on the instance and not on the Trove server. This file is sent to the guest instance by the trove-taskmanager service using cloud-init.

Please edit the file as shown next, by setting the auth_url and rabbit_host, userid, and password:

```
[DEFAULT]
log_file = trove-guestagent.log
log_dir = /var/log/trove/
ignore_users = os_admin
control_exchange = trove
trove_auth_url = http://172.22.6.246:35357/v3
nova_proxy_admin_pass =
nova_proxy_admin_tenant_name = trove
nova_proxy_admin_user = radmin
rabbit_password = rabb1tpwd
rabbit_host = 10.1.10.1
rabbit_userid = stackrabbit
```

Initializing the Trove database

After the configuration changes have been made, we will initialize the Trove database by executing the commands.

```
trove-manage db_sync
```

```
trove-manage datastore_upgrade mysql
```

This pushes the schema to the Trove database that was created during the installation phase. If we were to log in to the MySQL database that we created for Trove and take a look at it, we will now see that the tables are populated as shown in the following screenshot:

```
mysql> use trove;
Reading table information for completion of table and column names
You can turn off this feature to get a quicker startup with -A

Database changed
mysql> show tables;
+-------------------------------------------+
| Tables_in_trove                           |
+-------------------------------------------+
| agent_heartbeats                          |
| backups                                   |
| capabilities                              |
| capability_overrides                      |
| clusters                                  |
| conductor_lastseen                        |
| configuration_parameters                  |
| configurations                            |
| datastore_configuration_parameters        |
| datastore_version_metadata                |
| datastore_versions                        |
| datastores                                |
| dns_records                               |
| instances                                 |
| migrate_version                           |
| quota_usages                              |
| quotas                                    |
```

Restarting the services

Once the configuration has been completed, we need to restart all the services.

```
sudo service trove-api restart
```

```
sudo service trove-taskmanager restart
```

```
sudo service trove-conductor restart
```

This method will add the Trove project to an existing production installation running on the Ubuntu OpenStack distribution.

Summary

In this chapter, we have looked at the installation of Trove in a production environment and configuring Trove.

In the next chapter, we will learn how to create the guest images that we would use in either the DevStack environment or the production install.

Preparing the Guest Images

Now that the Trove system is installed, the next step is to build the images that we will use for the DBaaS to function properly. This is possibly the most important step as this will be the gold standard that Trove will use for a particular data store.

For the sake of simplicity and especially for testing, we can use the prebuilt images that are available from OpenStack itself. These images should strictly be used for testing and development use and should not be used in a production environment. The images are available for download and are located at `http://tarballs.openstack.org/trove/images/ubuntu/`.

In order to use the images from the preceding repository, we can only use the `10.0.0.0/24` subnet in the `FIXED_RANGE` of DevStack. This is because of the fact that the default gateway for these images is set to `10.0.0.1`.

In our case, we have used `10.1.10.0/24`, so the default gateway needs to be `10.1.10.1`. Hence, the images cannot be used directly. We have two options to use the prebuilt images:

- Run the `~/devstack/unstack.sh` script and remove the DevStack install, change the `FIXED_RANGE` variable, and rerun the `~/devstack/stack.sh` script
- Use guestfish to modify the default gateway of the images before uploading them to the `Glance` repository

We would, however, recommend you create a new image using **Disk Image Builder (DIB)** by following the instructions in this chapter.

For use with production systems, it is recommended to create our own images; that way, we can conform to standards set by the company's security team. We will also deal with creating the DIB elements that you can use to install other components.

Structure of a guest image

A guest image is technically just another Nova template on which some additional customization has been performed. The guest image technically has to fulfill the following aspects:

- It should have an operating system, and a database engine (installed or the ability to install it) format that Trove supports
- It should be in a format that Nova can boot – which means it should be of the same format of the hypervisor that we are trying to use with Nova
- It should have the Trove guest agent installed (or a way to install and configure the Trove guest agent)

The image, like all the other OpenStack images, will be stored in Glance so that it can be called and used by Nova and finally by Trove to orchestrate and manage the database engine that will be installed in the system itself.

As we have already seen in the previous chapters, the guest agent is different for different database engines, and hence the correct version of the guest agent needs to be installed on the system.

The images that are available for testing from the previously mentioned URL don't come with an installed guest agent, but they do so during boot time. This was done intentionally so that any changes are reflected quickly without us having to build the guest image if we change the configuration of the guest agent.

We should also remember that one image can only house one guest agent at the moment, and hence if we have to create two Trove data stores, we need to create two images. Also, images need to be created per hypervisor type if multi-hypervisor deployment is being used in OpenStack. as shown in the following:

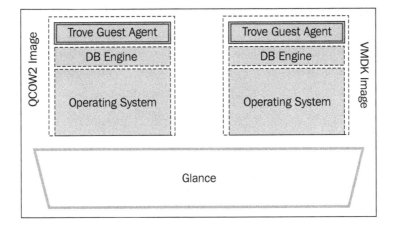

In order to understand the images and why they are created in the way that they are, let us take a look at the way the boot Trove images behave in the system. In order to check this, we will see exactly what happens when a `trove create` command is executed.

The `trove create` command is used to spin up a database instance. We will see the details of the command and the options later in this book, but for now, let's take a look at the sample command.

```
trove create <name> <flavor id> --size <Disk Volumes> --datastore
<Database engine name> --datastore_version <version>
```

Instance creation using the guest image

Once we run the command, the following steps are executed and the Trove instance is requested:

1. The Trove API service authenticates with Keystone and gets the token.

2. The Trove API validates the Trove flavor to check if it is valid.

3. The Trove API hands off to the task manager with a `Create Instance` API call after generating a unique identifier for the Trove database instance.

4. The task manager prepares the file for injection. There are two files:

    ◦   `trove-guestagent.conf`: This has the guest agent configuration with the Trove, RabbitMQ's URL, and user credentials alongside the Keystone URL – we configured this file in the previous chapter

    ◦   `guest_info.conf`: This file is generated and has three major things:

        ◦   The `guest_id`: This is actually the unique identifier generated by the Trove API

        ◦   The datastore manager: This is the database type that will be used

        ◦   `Tenant ID`: The Keystone tenant ID

5. The task manager, along with the files, sends the API command to Nova to boot the guest image.

6. Nova locates the image in Glance and creates an instance from it.

7. The Nova subsystem uses cloud-init to inject the files into the system.

8. Cinder volumes are added and mounted to the server.

9. The task manager creates a Guest queue in the AMQP system and leaves a `prepare` message.

10. The guest agent comes up and connects to the Guest queue (it connects to the right queue because of the injected files).

11. The guest agent picks up the `prepare` message and creates the database. The following functions are performed:

    ◦   The guest agent checks if the database engine is available on the system. If not, it executes a command to install the agent.

    ◦   The guest agent mounts the cinder volume and partitions the newly detected drive.

    ◦   The guest agent moves the data directory for the database engine to the newly mounted cinder volume

    ◦   The guest agent copies the default configuration of the database engine.

    ◦   The guest agent starts the database service.

12. The guest agent starts sending out periodic heartbeat messages to the Trove conductor, which updates them in the Trove database.

 The Trove task manager also keeps updating the Trove database with the status message.

Armed with the preceding information, we are now ready to create the image for Trove.

Creating the Trove guest image

We can use any method that we are comfortable with to create the Trove guest image. We need to just bear in mind some simple points:

- Cinder volumes will be added to the instance
- The partitioning of the new volume is also handled by Trove
- The database mount points are moved to the Cinder volume
- The software should be installed on the root volume

cloud-init is used to copy the `guest_info` file and guest agent configuration file. More often than not, it has problems with replacing files, so avoid keeping similar-named files in the destination.

The next decision that we have to take is between smaller initial boot time and a large number of images or a longer boot time with fewer images in the repository.

In order to explain the preceding, consider the following example of having to support two different data stores (MySQL and MongoDB).

On the images, we need to install the databases themselves. If we pre-install these, the boot times will be less as the guest agent can immediately come up and run its magic.

On the other hand, if we are ok to have the initial boot time on the higher side, we can install the database engine on the first boot.

Keeping all of this information in mind, installation approaches can be classified into two major categories:

- Installation using configuration management systems
- Installation using templates

Installation using configuration management systems

If your templates use configuration management systems like Chef, Puppet, CFEngine, and so on, we can just use the templates but set up the configuration management system to perform the following tasks:

- Install database engine (MySQL, Percona, and so on)
- Install the guest agent
- Start the guest agent

Installing the guest agent would also suffice, considering the fact that the guest agent can install the database engine if it has access to the repositories (internal/Internet). If you also recollect, the configuration files would already have been injected using the `cloud-init` script. So once the guest agent starts, it can straight away go to step 10 shown in the previous diagram; that is, connect to the message queue and start processing the prepare message.

This approach will work for any hypervisor image as this is independent of the image and acts completely outside the system. The obvious advantage of this approach is that the same system could work for different flavors of the operating systems and different databases as most configuration management systems allow for recipes to be configured on a per operating-system basis. This means that we can reuse our Nova images, install the guest images, and convert them for use with Trove.

The downside of this method is that it will take slightly more time than the template method, but this can be offset a little by having a local repository so that the Internet bandwidth and availability doesn't impact the provisioning time drastically.

Installation using templates

Installation using templates is fairly similar, but this increases the overhead in the management of templates. The advantage is that it is extremely fast when compared to the previous method.

In order to create the images for KVM/QEMU, we can use two methods:

- Disk Image Builder
- Red stack

These methods output images in the qcow2 format, which can be used with these hypervisors; however, qcow2 can also be converted into VMDK format to work with VMware hypervisors if we so choose. We could also use methods such as SUSE Studio among others.

Disk Image Builder

This is by far the most commonly used method to create Trove images. It was created by HP and NTT Docomo to create images. The **Disk Image Builder (DIB)** system works on the construct of elements, which are nothing but scripts in a certain order to build the system.

Installing the DIB

No installation is required for the DIB. It can be run directly from source and hence in order to use it, we will clone the repository and use it.

```
sudo apt-get install qemu-utils kpartx

cd /opt/stack

git clone https://git.openstack.org/openstack/diskimage-builder
```

> If you are using an HTTP proxy, we will use the methods mentioned in the previous chapters to configure apt-get and git to use the proxies.

```
Cloning into 'diskimage-builder'...
remote: Counting objects: 12511, done.
remote: Compressing objects: 100% (6307/6307), done.
remote: Total 12511 (delta 7132), reused 10088 (delta 5167)
Receiving objects: 100% (12511/12511), 1.99 MiB | 239.00 KiB/s, done.
Resolving deltas: 100% (7132/7132), done.
Checking connectivity... done.
alokas@DevStack:/opt/stack$
```

The repository is cloned; we can see the DIB elements by navigating to the directory.

```
cd diskimage-builder/elements
```

A directory list command will show us all the elements.

```
alokas@DevStack:/opt/stack$ cd diskimage-builder/elements/
alokas@DevStack:/opt/stack/diskimage-builder/elements$ ls
apt-conf                          hpdsa
apt-preferences                   hwburnin
apt-sources                       hwdiscovery
architecture-emulation-binaries   ilo
baremetal                         install-static
base                              install-types
bootloader                        ironic-agent
cache-url                         ironic-discoverd-ramdisk
centos                            iso
centos7                           local-config
```

Each of the elements is a directory and has a folder structure, with some child directories. We will discuss these in a bit more detail in the next section.

We will then install the DIB utilities.

```
cd /opt/stack
git clone https://github.com/openstack/dib-utils.git
cd dib-utils
 ./setup.py build
sudo ./setup.py install
```

This will provide the utilities to DIB, and is normally installed during the Trove install components. However, if we are using a proxy, this step will fail and so will the creation of the image, hence we have installed it manually.

Basic working of the DIB

The DIB creates a chroot in which it creates the images. As you already know, it performs activities sequentially and the order of the scripts is as follows:

- `root.d`: The first set of scripts to run outside the chroot environment.
- `extra-data.d`: Used to copy data from outside the chroot to inside the chroot environment. All the steps after this run inside the chroot.
- `pre-install.d`: Runs the pre-provisioning script.
- `install.d`: Runs the install script.
- `post-install.d`: Runs the post-provisioning script.

- `block-device.d`: Runs outside the chroot environment and is used to configure the block devices.
- `finalise.d`: Final steps.
- `cleanup.d`: Cleans up after finishing its work.

Although all these scripts are available, not all of them may be used in the elements.

Installing Trove-integration scripts and TripleO

The basic DIB templates don't have all the information for creating the Trove image. Hence, we need to also get some additional scripts from the trove-integration project. This is again done by cloning a `git` repository.

```
cd /opt/stack
git clone https://github.com/openstack/trove-integration.git
git clone https://git.openstack.org/openstack/tripleo-image-elements.git
```

```
Cloning into 'trove-integration'...
remote: Counting objects: 5202, done.
remote: Total 5202 (delta 0), reused 0 (delta 0), pack-reused 5202
Receiving objects: 100% (5202/5202), 1.97 MiB | 192.00 KiB/s, done.
Resolving deltas: 100% (2965/2965), done.
Checking connectivity... done.
alokas@DevStack:/opt/stack$
```

The DIB elements are located in the `trove-integration/scripts/files/elements` directory.

```
alokas@DevStack:/opt/stack/trove-integration/scripts/files/elements$ ls
fedora-guest     fedora-postgresql  ubuntu-db2       ubuntu-percona
fedora-mariadb   fedora-redis       ubuntu-guest     ubuntu-postgresql
fedora-mongodb   ubuntu-cassandra   ubuntu-mariadb   ubuntu-pxc
fedora-mysql     ubuntu-couchbase   ubuntu-mongodb   ubuntu-redis
fedora-percona   ubuntu-couchdb     ubuntu-mysql     ubuntu-vertica
alokas@DevStack:/opt/stack/trove-integration/scripts/files/elements$
```

As you can see, this folder has the elements that will install different databases on the different operating systems. (We have elements for Fedora and Ubuntu.) We shall be using Ubuntu-MySQL for our purposes.

SSH keys

If we don't already have the SSH keys generated and added to the `authorized_keys` section, it should be done now.

```
ssh-keygen -t rsa -b 4096
```

Choose the defaults and this will generate `key-pair`, `id_rsa`, and `id_rsa.pub`. `authorized_keys` need to be updated using the public key. This is required as we need to be able to send the keys into the image for us to be able to log in to the Trove instance later. We can choose not to do this, but then we won't be able to SSH into the instance for troubleshooting.

```
cat ~/.ssh/id_rsa.pub >> ~/.ssh/authorized_keys"
```

We will change the permissions on the directories as expected.

```
chmod 755 ~/.ssh
chmod 644 ~/.ssh/authorized_keys
```

Install Percona keys (only if using proxies)

There is a script that runs in the pre-install phase of MySQL, MariaDB, and Percona install. This sets the Percona keys and repositories. However, if we are using the `apt-key` command, we have to pass the proxies explicitly.

Please follow this only if you are using a web proxy. If the system you are using for the disk building has direct Internet access, then this step needs to be ignored.

The following commands show the changes that are required in case of MySQL, but the same will be applicable in other cases as well.

We will take a backup of the file.

```
cp /opt/stack/trove-integration/scripts/files/elements/ubuntu-mysql/pre-install.d/10-percona-apt-key \
/opt/stack/trove-integration/scripts/files/elements/ubuntu-mysql/pre-install.d/10-percona-apt-key.old
```

Execute the following command to modify the `apt-key` command in the script. Please replace `172.21.2.17:80` with your proxy IP and port.

```
sed -i "s%apt-key adv%apt-key adv --keyserver-options \
http-proxy=http://172.21.2.17:80%g" "/opt/stack/trove-integration/
scripts/files/elements/ubuntu-mysql/pre-install.d/10-percona-apt-key"
```

A simple `diff` command should show that the `http-proxy` command parameters have been added.

```
alokas@DevStack /opt/stack
alokas@DevStack:/opt/stack$ diff "/opt/stack/trove-integration/scripts/files/elements/ubunt
u-mysql/pre-install.d/10-percona-apt-key" "/opt/stack/trove-integration/scripts/files/eleme
nts/ubuntu-mysql/pre-install.d/10-percona-apt-key.old"
15c15
< apt-key adv --keyserver-options http-proxy=http://172.21.2.17:80 --keyserver hkp://keys.g
nupg.net --recv-keys 1C4CBDCDCD2EFD2A
---
> apt-key adv --keyserver hkp://keys.gnupg.net --recv-keys 1C4CBDCDCD2EFD2A
alokas@DevStack:/opt/stack$
```

Creating your own DIB elements (optional)

One of the things that we may want to do is to create our own DIB elements in order to install some additional components or even to change the way the installation works. Although the scripts that can be used are beyond the scope of this book, we shall take a look at the basics of how one could achieve it.

Since we have already seen the structure of the DIB elements in the previous sections of this chapter, in order to create a DIB element ourselves, we could copy a folder structure of any existing DIB elements and replace the scripts with our own. As an example, installing the `nagios-nrpe` agent on the system so that we can add it to Nagios monitoring after the database instance spins up.

We will copy the directory structure of an existing DIB element to a new folder; in this case, we choose to use `ubuntu-mysql`.

```
mkdir -p /opt/stack/trove-integration/scripts/files/nagios-nrpe
```

```
cp -r /opt/stack/trove-integration/scripts/files/elements/ubuntu-mysql/*
/opt/stack/trove-integration/scripts/files/nagios-nrpe/
```

Once the new folder is populated, we can now delete the files we don't need. We will execute the command:

```
cd /opt/stack/trove-integration/scripts/files/nagios-nrpe
```

```
find . -name "*" -type f -delete
```

This will leave the directory structure but delete the files inside it. Please ensure the delete is suffixed and not prefixed or everything will be deleted.

We can now execute the `ls` command and verify that the files are indeed deleted. We chose this particular DIB element because it has only two elements: `preinstall.d` and `install.d`.

We will need only `install.d` in this case. We will now create the install script that is executed inside the chroot environment.

```
cd install.d
cat <<EOF > 10-install-nrpe
#!/bin/bash
cd /tmp
wget https://assets.nagios.com/downloads/nagiosxi/agents/linux-nrpe-agent.tar.gz
tar xzf linux-nrpe-agent.tar.gz
cd linux-nrpe-agent
sudo ./fullinstall

EOF
```

This will create the script to install `nrpe`. We will then change that to executable by using the command:

```
chmod 755 10-install-nrpe
```

This element can now be used and it will install the NRPE agent in the image. We can use this to run our own scripts to install several components on the images. We just have to put the element name (in our case `nagios-nrpe`) and the element will be added.

In order to get more details on developing different DIB elements and debugging them, please refer to `http://docs.openstack.org/developer/diskimage-builder/developer/developing_elements.html`.

Creating images using the DIB

The image creation process is a simple command in the DIB, where we pass the name of the elements to install in a certain order. However, some preparatory work needs to be done before the command can be executed.

Exporting environment variables

Before we can execute the command, we need to export some variables. The absence of these means the script will fail.

- `HOST_USERNAME`: The OS username that is on the Trove server; this is used to identify the right keys/SSH keys and the `authorized_keys` file.

- `HOST_SCP_USERNAME`: The username used to copy the guest agent.

- GUEST_USERNAME: The username that will run the guest agent on the Trove guest machine.

- NETWORK_GATEWAY: The IP of the Trove controller node. This would be set to 10.0.0.1 in the prebuilt images and that's why they can't be used straightaway in this book/another environment where the IP ranges are different.

- REDSTACK_SCRIPTS: The Location where the Trove integration project is downloaded.

- PATH_TROVE: The path where Trove source files are kept in the Trove controller node.

- ESCAPED_PATH_TROVE: Same as the preceding, but the slashes are escaped.

- SSH_DIR: The location where authorized_keys, id_rsa, and id_rsa.pub files are placed on the Trove controller node.

- GUEST_LOGDIR: The location where the log file needs to be created.

- ESCAPED_GUEST_LOGDIR: Same as the preceding, but the slashes are escaped.

- DIB_CLOUD_INIT_DATASOURCES: Used to determine where the metadata for the instance needs to be obtained.

- ELEMENTS_PATH: This needs to have the TripleO elements path and Trove integration script.

- RELEASE: The Ubuntu release version; since we are using 14.04, we will use trusty as the value.

We will export these using values for our environment. In the production environment, not much other than the usernames and network gateway would change.

```
export HOST_USERNAME=alokas
export HOST_SCP_USERNAME=alokas
export GUEST_USERNAME=ubuntu
export NETWORK_GATEWAY=10.1.10.1
export REDSTACK_SCRIPTS=/opt/stack/trove-integration/scripts
export PATH_TROVE=/opt/stack/trove
export ESCAPED_PATH_TROVE='\/opt\/stack\/trove'
export SSH_DIR=/home/alokas/.ssh
export GUEST_LOGDIR=/var/log/trove/
export ESCAPED_GUEST_LOGDIR='\/var\/log\/trove\/'
export DIB_CLOUD_INIT_DATASOURCES='ConfigDrive'
export RELEASE=trusty
export ELEMENTS_PATH=/opt/stack/trove-integration/scripts/files/
elements:/opt/stack/tripleo-image-elements/elements
```

Building the QCOW2 image

Once the variables have been exported, we can execute the disk-image-create command in order to generate the image.

 In a production system, we would typically not be using the i386 architecture as this will cause performance degradation. However, we use it here as we are running a nested virtualization (for the purposes of this book) and the hypervisor that's installed is QEMU for 32 bit.

The command is shown next:

```
cd /opt/stack
diskimage-builder/bin/disk-image-create -a i386 \
-o /home/alokas/images/ubuntu_mysql/ubuntu_mysql -x \
--qemu-img-options compat=0.10 ubuntu vm heat-cfntools cloud-init-
datasources \
ubuntu-guest ubuntu-mysql
```

 If we need to know the command format and the options available, we can execute /opt/stack/diskimage-builder/bin/disk-image-create --help.

This will print the command help.

Usage: disk-image-create [OPTION]... [ELEMENT]...

The image-create command that we are using functions in the following way:

- We set the architecture to create a 32 bit image using -a i386.
- We set the output file path by using -o /home/alokas/images/ubuntu_mysql.
- We set the tracing on using the -x option.
- We set the QEMU Image Options (compat=0.10) to mention that we want a QEMU version 2 image and not the version 3 image.

- We then mention the elements that we need to install – these are all the elements that are picked from the base DIB elements and also the trove-integration project. We can choose to create new elements and include them in the list if we want more software installed on our image:
    - Ubuntu
    - vm
    - heat-cfntools
    - cloud-init-datasources
    - Ubuntu-guest
    - Ubuntu-mysql

If the guest needs to connect to the Internet using the proxy, then the `local-settings` element can be used to set the proxy and SSH keys.

You could take a look at all the elements (by looking at the scripts in their individual directories); however, we will take a look at the `ubuntu-mysql` element. This element is provided by the `trove-integration` package and is located at `/opt/stack/trove-integration/scripts/files/elements/ubuntu-mysql`. We will look inside the directory in the `install.d` folder.

We find the `30-mysql` script, which does the actual install of MySQL. Looking at the script (only the relevant part being shown next):

```
#!/bin/sh

. . .

apt-get -y install libmysqlclient18 mysql-server-5.6 percona-
xtrabackup-22

. . .
```

We can see that it installs mysql-server version 5.6. If you have a different version of that script, the version might be different. If you need to change the version that is installed, you can change this line before running the DIB command.

Once the command is executed, you will see a whole lot of information of what the system is actually doing at the moment. This will include downloading software from the Internet and executing the install scripts.

Since access to the Internet is required, please ensure that the proxy variables are set (if they are needed). Also ensure that you have set the proxy in the Percona repository or anywhere else where the keys might be needed. We have not used the element that we created as that is not needed at the moment for our purposes.

At the end of it, you should see an image created.

```
alokas@DevStack:~$ cd ~/images/ubuntu_mysql
alokas@DevStack:~/images/ubuntu_mysql$ ls -lh
total 483M
drwxrwxr-x 3 alokas alokas 4.0K Dec 20 00:17 ubuntu_mysql.d
-rw-r--r-- 1 alokas alokas 484M Dec 20 00:18 ubuntu_mysql.qcow2
alokas@DevStack:~/images/ubuntu_mysql$
```

This image is now ready to be used for the Trove system.

Red stack scripts

The name for scripts can be traced back to the time when Trove was called the Red Dwarf. They have a fairly simple installation process for Ubuntu. The scripts were installed when we installed the Trove-integration package. If you have not downloaded the package, refer to the section *Installing Trove-integration scripts and TripleO* earlier in the chapter. We will also need to perform the exporting of the environment variables as we did in the DIB install.

cd /opt/stack/trove-integration/scripts

./redstack build-image mysql

We can replace mysql in the preceding command with percona, mongodb, redis, Cassandra, couchbase, postgresql, couchdb to create the image for these database engines. The scripts also set up a DevStack environment; hence, we won't be using this method. But we have shown it just for the sake of completeness.

Uploading the Trove images

Once we have created the guest images, we now need to perform the Trove operations to upload the images and register them with the Trove system for it to be usable.

We will export the credentials as we have done in the past.

cd ~

export OS_TENANT_NAME=admin

```
export OS_AUTH_URL=http://172.22.6.246:5000/v2.0

export OS_USERNAME=admin

export OS_PASSWORD=adm1npwd
```

Once this is done, we will execute the command `trove datastore-list`. At this point in time, it will come up as empty as we have not registered any data stores.

```
alokas@DevStack:~$ trove datastore-list
+-----+-------+
| ID | Name |
+-----+-------+
+-----+-------+
```

We will upload our newly created image as the `mysql` datastore. This needs the following steps:

1. Upload image to Glance.

2. Create the Trove datastore using the `trove-manage` command:

```
glance image-create --name mysql  \
--disk-format qcow2 \
--container-format bare --visibility public \
--file /home/alokas/images/ubuntu_mysql/ubuntu_mysql.qcow2
```

```
alokas@DevStack:~$ glance image-create --name mysql  \
> --disk-format qcow2 \
> --container-format bare --visibility public \
> --file /home/alokas/images/ubuntu_mysql/ubuntu_mysql.qcow2

+------------------+--------------------------------------+
| Property         | Value                                |
+------------------+--------------------------------------+
| checksum         | 71dd35ca5d659f41e882a624078ee270     |
| container_format | bare                                 |
| created_at       | 2015-12-20T06:43:23Z                 |
| disk_format      | qcow2                                |
| id               | 49412d90-2580-4e25-a463-f232a517657b |
| min_disk         | 0                                    |
| min_ram          | 0                                    |
| name             | mysql                                |
| owner            | c02f0d1d442a4e32b49c5f4f6f769367     |
| protected        | False                                |
| size             | 507052032                            |
| status           | active                               |
| tags             | []                                   |
| updated_at       | 2015-12-20T06:43:34Z                 |
| virtual_size     | None                                 |
| visibility       | public                               |
+------------------+--------------------------------------+
```

We will note down the image ID, which in our case is **49412d90-2580-4e25-a463-f232a517657b**.

The image is now uploaded. As the next step, we will create a data store for `mysql` and then subsequently add a version.

```
trove-manage datastore_update mysql ''
```

```
alokas@DevStack:~$ trove-manage datastore_update mysql ''
2015-12-20 01:46:10.321 INFO trove.db.sqlalchemy.session [-]
h args: {'pool_recycle': 3600, 'echo': False}
Datastore 'mysql' updated.
```

This creates the mysql data store. We will now update the version and other parameters.

```
trove-manage datastore_version_update mysql 5.6 \
```

```
mysql 49412d90-2580-4e25-a463-f232a517657b \
```

```
"mysql-server-5.6" 1
```

Please note that we are using version 5.6, as the ubuntu-mysql element installs MySQL version 5.6. The guest agent, while booting, checks for the database version that is installed on the instance and the one requested in the data store version, and if a different version is installed, then it tries to install the right version. This feature allows us to install the database during the first boot process. This is fine when it comes to an upgrade, but in case of a downgrade, the system may not be able to handle it, so it's recommended that the data store version be the same as the version already installed in the image so as to avoid failure.

Let us take a look at the command and what it means:

- The datastore name is `mysql`.

- The version of the data store is 5.6.

- The manager of the datastore is MySQL – Trove guest agent has manager classes for the different data stores that it supports; normally, it is the name of the database itself. Here is a list of all the manager names and their class names:

Manager name	Trove class
Percona	`trove.guestagent.datastore.mysql.manager.Manager`
Redis	`trove.guestagent.datastore.experimental.redis.manager.Manager`

Manager name	Trove class
Cassandra	`trove.guestagent.datastore.experimental.` `cassandra.manager.Manager`
Couchbase	`trove.guestagent.datastore.experimental.` `couchbase.manager.Manager`
MongoDB	`trove.guestagent.datastore.experimental.mongodb.` `manager.Manager`
PostgreSQL	`trove.guestagent.datastore.experimental.` `postgresql.manager.Manager`
Vertica	`trove.guestagent.datastore.experimental.vertica.` `manager.Manager`
DB2	`trove.guestagent.datastore.experimental.db2.` `manager.Manager`
MySQL	`trove.guestagent.datastore.mysql.manager.Manager`

- The unique ID mentioned is the image ID from Glance (that we noted down earlier).
- The next parameter is the user-friendly name.
- The final one is to set the active flag to `true`.

Once the command completes successfully, we should be able to execute the `trove datastore-list` command and we should see the output.

```
alokas@DevStack:~$ trove datastore-list
+----------------------------------------+-------+
| ID                                     | Name  |
+----------------------------------------+-------+
| ea4ac33c-83e9-4ed8-8cf8-5124f181e4ba   | mysql |
+----------------------------------------+-------+
```

Modify QCOW2 images using guestfish

If we want to modify the QCOW2 image that we have just created or the one that is downloaded from the Internet, without booting, we could do so by using the guestfish utility. This is provided by the `libguestfs` library.

Installing guestfish

The installation of guestfish is fairly simple.

```
apt-get install libguestfs-tools
```

On some versions (like 12.04), the command is `apt-get install guestfish`. It will also ask for the creation of the virtual appliance; please do so. Once the appliance is installed, you can then execute the command `sudo guestfish` (or as root).

Loading the images

Once in the guestfish console, you can then load the qcow2 image by typing the command `add <full path to qcow2 imange>`.

```
add /home/alokas/mysql.qcow2
```

We will then type the command `run`, which will load the image.

```
alokas@DevStack:~$ sudo guestfish

Welcome to guestfish, the guest filesystem shell for
editing virtual machine filesystems and disk images.

Type: 'help' for help on commands
      'man' to read the manual
      'quit' to quit the shell

><fs>  add /home/alokas/mysql.qcow2
><fs> run
 75%                                                           00:03
 100%                                                          00:00
><fs>
```

Once the slider reaches 100%, we are ready to proceed further.

Modify the files on the image

We can mount the volumes that are available in the image; we can execute the command `list-filesystems`.

```
><fs> list-filesystems
/dev/sda1: ext4
```

We can now mount the volume using the command format `mount <volume name> <mount point>`.

```
mount /dev/sda1 /
```

Once the filesystem is mounted, we can modify the files at our will by using `vi`; for example, to modify the SSH configuration (`vi /etc/ssh/sshd_config`).

We could also mount the filesystem as read only if we don't want to accidentally make changes.

Send commands

We can also send commands to guestfish. However, care should be taken that the command doesn't have user interactions or the guestfish shell will freeze.

The command format is `command "bash -c '<command to be passed>'"`.

Example: Adding a user to the Ubuntu QCOW2 image

For example, we need to add a user (testuser) to an Ubuntu system with the password `test123` and add it to the sudoers group, so we can log in using the console (or SSH if the SSH configuration is modified to allow it). We will first generate the password hash using perl (outside of guestfish).

```
pass=$(perl -e 'print crypt($ARGV[0], "password")' "test123")
```

This will store the hash in a variable called `pass`; we will check the output by `echo $pass`, and we have to note down this hash (in our case, this is **paOElDH7voHBo**).

```
alokas@DevStack:~$ pass=$(perl -e 'print crypt($ARGV[0], "password")' "test123")
alokas@DevStack:~$ echo $pass
paOElDH7voHBo
alokas@DevStack:~$
```

We will then use the command format of guestfish and execute.

```
><fs>
><fs> command "bash -c 'useradd -m -p paOElDH7voHBo testuser'"

><fs> command "bash -c 'usermod -a -G sudo testuser'"
```

This will add the user **testuser** with the password **test123**. Using the `quit` command, we can get out of the shell and use the modified image. For more information, read the manual using the `man guestfish` command.

Summary

After going through the chapter, we should now have a basic idea of how the images in Trove are different from the base Nova images.

Now that all the basic building blocks are in place, in the next chapter, we will start with the real action in terms of actually provisioning instances.

5
Provisioning Database Instances

At this juncture, we are ready to provision our first database instance. We will use the image that we created in the previous chapter. In case you did not create an image in the previous chapter, we could also use the test images that we can download from `http://tarballs.openstack.org/trove/images/ubuntu/` (see previous chapter for details) or get other images purpose built for OpenStack Trove provided by companies like Tesora.

Checking for prerequisites

So, now that we are ready to provision, we need to check that the system has all that it needs to provision a database instance for us.

We will quickly check the following:

- **Flavors available**: We can check this by using the command `trove flavor-list`, which will essentially show us the flavors and the nova instance sizes where the database will be running. We will need this information while launching new Trove instances. We will need the ID from these for whichever flavor we want to launch. The flavors simply show us the flavors defined in the nova subsystem and can also be seen using the `nova flavor-list` command.

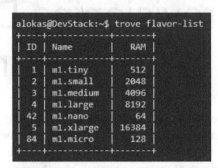

- **Datastore available**: This is essentially which image to boot from. We created the MySQL image in the last chapter, so this should be available for us. This can be verified by the command `trove datastore-list`.

- **Datastore versions available**: We will also need to check that at least one datastore version is available for the datastore. We will execute the command:

```
trove Datastore-version-list <ID of Datastore>
```

```
alokas@DevStack:~$ trove datastore-version-list \
> e76bcc91-1375-4b8a-8acb-642959c4acd9
+--------------------------------------+------+
| ID                                   | Name |
+--------------------------------------+------+
| 6550c959-8a8a-4f6b-ad10-dd1c23f5ec52 | 5.6  |
+--------------------------------------+------+
```

The other things to check will be if the hypervisor has enough space in order to provision the instances, whether cinder has enough space to provide for the volume, and finally if the tenant that we are using has available quotas, all of which we can check from the dashboard.

Launching our first instance

We will launch our first Trove instance with one simple command. We will discuss the command format in detail in the coming section. However, the simplest command will need the following information:

- **Flavor ID**: The ID of the flavor. Say we are spinning up an `m1.small`, we will use the ID 2.

- **Name**: This will be the name of the instance; you can choose it to describe the instance. In our case, let us say `mytest`.

- **Size of the volume**: As we have discussed earlier in the book, Trove installs and moves the data volumes to the cinder volume. Therefore, we will need to provide the size for it.

- **Datastore**: The name of the datastore, in our case MySQL.

- **Datastore version**: The version of the datastore, in our case 5.6.

Now that we have all the information we need, let us take a look at the command:

```
trove create mytest 2 --size 1 --datastore mysql --datastore_version 5.6
```

This will return the ID of the instance being created.

```
+---------------------+--------------------------------------+
| Property            | Value                                |
+---------------------+--------------------------------------+
| created             | 2016-01-06T03:10:39                  |
| datastore           | mysql                                |
| datastore_version   | 5.6                                  |
| flavor              | 2                                    |
| id                  | 879dcf19-8fd6-4044-9a4c-30577b5b52dd |
| name                | mytest                               |
| status              | BUILD                                |
| updated             | 2016-01-06T03:10:39                  |
| volume              | 1                                    |
+---------------------+--------------------------------------+
```

This instance will be ready in a while; we can track the progress using the `trove list` command. The system will first request nova to create an instance using the glance image and then wait for the guest agent to boot up, connect to the queue, pick up the message, and connect to `trove-taskmanager` to work its magic.

There are several other options you can use and pass in the command-line options (type `trove help create` to see the options and the descriptions).

```
alokas@DevStack:~$ trove help create
usage: trove create <name> <flavor>
                     [--size <size>] [--volume_type <volume_type>]
                     [--databases <databases> [<databases> ...]]
                     [--users <users> [<users> ...]] [--backup <backup>]
                     [--availability_zone <availability_zone>]
                     [--datastore <datastore>]
                     [--datastore_version <datastore_version>]
                     [--nic <net-id=net-uuid,v4-fixed-ip=ip-addr,port-id=port-uuid>]
                     [--configuration <configuration>]
                     [--replica_of <source_instance>] [--replica_count <count>]

Creates a new instance.

Positional arguments:
  <name>                    Name of the instance.
  <flavor>                  Flavor ID or name of the instance.
```

Let's take a look at what is happening under the covers while the system is being built. We would like to bring to your attention a diagram that we saw in the previous chapter. The following is a snippet of the diagram that we saw previously:

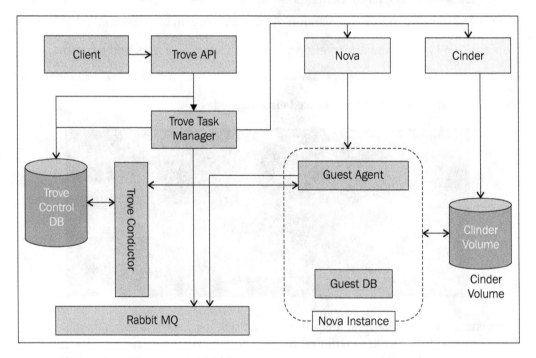

The broad steps in the creation phase are the following:

1. The **Trove API** receives the request and passes it along to the task manager.

2. The **Trove Task Manager** makes API calls to **Nova** and **Cinder** to create an instance, a volume, and mounts the volume on the instance.

3. The **Trove Task Manager** then leaves a `prepare` message in the RabbitMQ.

4. The **Guest Agent** boots on the guest instance and retrieves the prepare message and installs and/or configures the database engine and starts it.

In the preceding diagram, the `trove create` command has put the trove instance in the build state. We will now execute the commands `nova list` and `cinder list` to see what is happening.

The Trove task manager makes the API calls to the instance and the cinder volume to:

• Create the nova instance

• Create the cinder volume

• Attach the cinder volume to the Nova instance

• Boot the nova instance

The following output from `nova list` shows the machine is getting provisioned:

We need to notice a few points here:

• The **ID** of the nova instance is different from that of the Trove instance, which is because trove effectively is the superset and represents the whole nine yards (including nova instance, cinder volume, guest agent, and so on).

• **Power State** is **NOSTATE** and machine state is **BUILD**. We can see that **block_device_mapping** is the current task, which essentially means the cinder volume is being created and mounted on the instance.

A simple `cinder list` will confirm this.

```
alokas@DevStack:~$ cinder list
+-------------+--------+------------------+------------------+------+-------------+----------+-------------+-------------+
|     ID      | Status | Migration Status |       Name       | Size | Volume Type | Bootable | Multiattach | Attached to |
+-------------+--------+------------------+------------------+------+-------------+----------+-------------+-------------+
| 2e5d2e88-...| in-use |        -         | datastore-c0881..| 1    | lvmdriver-1 |  false   |    False    | 37d632c8-...|
+-------------+--------+------------------+------------------+------+-------------+----------+-------------+-------------+
```

Looking at the command, we should take notice of a few things:

- The size of the drive is the same value that we passed on to the `trove create` command (1 GB)
- The disk is non-bootable as this is going to be the data drive
- The multi-attach is set to off as it will be only associated to one instance at a time
- It's attached to the Nova instance

If we continue to execute the `nova list` command, the status will change from **BUILDING** to **ACTIVE** and the power state will change to **Running**.

Meanwhile, the Trove guest agent would have created a queue and left the Prepare message there. In order to view the message left in the AMQP queue, we will need the RabbitMQ management plugin.

The RabbitMQ management plugin can be installed on the system by using the command:

sudo rabbitmq-plugins enable rabbitmq_management

This enables the RabbitMQ management plugin, which can provide the GUI and CLI access to the message queue system. We will now need to restart the `rabbitmq-server` process.

sudo service rabbitmq-server restart

After this is completed, we should be able to log in to the GUI using the following URL: `http://172.22.6.246:15672/` (replace the IP address with the IP of the server running the DevStack instance). The username and password will be `guest` and `guest` respectively (unless you have changed it in the RabbitMQ configuration).

Look at all the queues tab and filter it with the ID of the Trove instance (in our case **879dcf19-8fd6-4044-9a4c-30577b5b52dd**).

You will see that the guest queue is created and has a message waiting to be read.

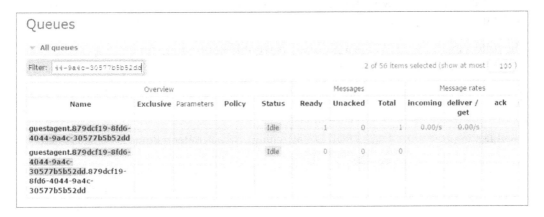

 We can read the message, but that may hamper the working of the system, because even if we set **Re-Queue** to `true`, the message will be marked as redelivered.

If we look at the queue, it will be cleared once the guest instance picks the message up. A sample message looks like this:

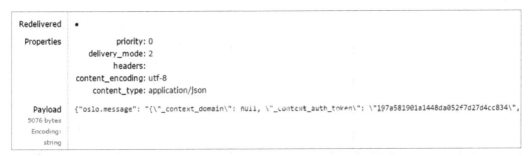

The message itself is a fairly long string of JSON and has the following information:

- Service context – with the endpoint URLs for services
- System configuration/information:
  - Device name and mount points (where the data directory is mounted)
  - RAM – RAM is required for the calculation of some values (as we will see in the next chapter) in the configuration
  - Root password for the MySQL database
- The configuration template for the database engine

With this information, the guest agent is able to configure the instance (as per the prepare call steps that were mentioned in the previous chapter) to the requirements of the user.

The following table provides a glimpse of what is happening depending on the state of the Trove instance and the underpinning Nova instance:

Trove state	Nova state – current task	Remarks
BUILD	BUILD – attaching block storage	The cinder volume is being created and mounted on the system.
BUILD	BUILD – spawning	The glance image is being copied to the hypervisor and booting up.
BUILD	ACTIVE	The nova instance and cinder volumes are ready. The OS is booting up on the instance and the Trove system is waiting for the guest agent to come up and process the Prepare message.
ERROR	ACTIVE	Something went wrong in the guest agent phase. Things to check: • guest agent properly installed • The appropriate datastore version installed/access to the Internet to install the same • Trove timing out before the guest agent can finish the process • Wrong guest agent configuration/default gateway/routing information
ERROR	ERROR	The Nova/Cinder/Glance system having some issues. Please troubleshoot the underpinning systems.
ACTIVE	ACTIVE	Everything was fine. The guest database is ready for use.

If all goes well, we would end up in the ACTIVE state of Trove, which means we can now hand off the system to the actual requestor.

However, if the DB creation errors out, we might want to take a look at the appropriate logs (dependent on where it errored out). At the present moment, we can only look at the guest-agent logs by logging into the instance using SSH (or using the VNC console, if we have set up user credentials). However, there is a blueprint that is completed and under review (expected to be published by the Mitaka-3 release) that will allow users to download the guest-agent logs without access to the instance. The link to this feature is `https://blueprints.launchpad.net/trove/+spec/datastore-log-operations`.

We finally take a look at the networking aspect of the Trove system. The networking is controlled by either the nova network (as it is in our case) or Neutron (if we were using neutron networking); however, Trove also dictates the creation and association of a security group by default.

Since this is the MySQL datastore, the Trove system creates a security group and allows port 3306 through the group.

Let's take a look at the output of `nova show< instance name>` (pay attention to the **security_groups** values).

```
alokas@DevStack:~$ nova show mytest
+-----------------------------+----------------------------------------+
| Property                    | Value                                  |
+-----------------------------+----------------------------------------+
| OS-DCF:diskConfig           | AUTO                                   |
| OS-EXT-AZ:availability_zone | nova                                   |
| OS-EXT-SRV-ATTR:host        | DevStack                               |
| OS-EXT-SRV-ATTR:hostname    | mytest                                 |
| security_groups             | SecGroup_37d632-...., default          |
| status                      | ACTIVE                                 |
| tenant_id                   | 1bc311ab6cf8443h87d95f93h926e93c       |
| updated                     | 2016-02-07T11:54:04Z                   |
| user_id                     | d31bc7aa749041bbb77d9ffe21d432fd       |
+-----------------------------+----------------------------------------+
```

We can see that there are two security groups associated. Let's now take a look at the rules allowed or denied by those security groups.

```
alokas@DevStack:~$ nova secgroup-list-rules SecGroup_37d632-.....
+--------------+-------------+-----------+-------------+---------------+
| IP Protocol | From Port   | To Port   | IP Range    | Source Group  |
+--------------+-------------+-----------+-------------+---------------+
| tcp          | 3306        | 3306      | 0.0.0.0/0   |               |
+--------------+-------------+-----------+-------------+---------------+
alokas@DevStack:~$
alokas@DevStack:~$ nova secgroup-list-rules default
+--------------+-------------+-----------+-------------+---------------+
| IP Protocol | From Port   | To Port   | IP Range    | Source Group  |
+--------------+-------------+-----------+-------------+---------------+
+--------------+-------------+-----------+-------------+---------------+
```

The commands to view the security groups will change if we are using Neutron. The corresponding neutron commands are neutron security-group-list and neutron security-group-show <security group name>.

The default security group will not come into play as it is empty. However, as per the default configuration in nova (allow_same_net_traffic), the same subnet traffic is not restricted using the security group. However, from the outside, only access to port 3306 is allowed unless explicitly allowed in the security group.

If you are wondering where the values for the TCP/UDP ports are to be opened for each datastore picked up, the answer is trove-taskmanager.conf (if the configuration options are not set, the default values are used – the defaults are stored in the file trove/common/cfg.py).

The following shows the configuration options that we can put in the trove-taskmanger.conf file and modify it to impact the security groups. For example, setting the tcp_ports setting for MySQL to 3306, 22 (from just 3306) will add the SSH port while creating the security group.

```
[mysql]
# Format (single port or port range): A, B-C
# where C greater than B
tcp_ports = 3306
[cassandra]
tcp_ports = 7000, 7001, 9042, 9160
[default]
trove_security_groups_support = True
```

In order to disable the creation of security groups completely, set the configuration option trove_security_groups_support to False in trove-taskmanager.conf.

This is not recommended in a production environment as this may open security risks to the database instances.

Logging into the instance via SSH

We can access the guest instance, either by using SSH or by using the VNC console; this is not necessary for the functioning of Trove.

 Please note that the security group will prevent access to SSH unless either a rule is added or the source server is on the same subnet.

In our case, we are executing SSH from the Trove controller system with the IP 10.1.10.1, which is in the same subnet, and nova.conf has an option called allow_same_net_traffic (which defaults to True) that has not been fiddled with in our case, so we should be able to SSH in.

One reason for logging in can be to troubleshoot a guest agent failure. We can log in to the instance (if you have created the image as shown in the previous chapter) using the private key that you created for your own user. (The Trove integration element also copies the authorized_keys file to the image.)

We can find details about the instance by using the command trove show <instance name/id>.

```
alokas@DevStack:~$ trove show mytest
+-------------------+------------------------------------------+
| Property          | Value                                    |
+-------------------+------------------------------------------+
| created           | 2016-01-06T03:10:39                      |
| datastore         | mysql                                    |
| datastore_version | 5.6                                      |
| flavor            | 2                                        |
| id                | 879dcf19-8fd6-4044-9a4c-30577b5b52dd     |
| ip                | 10.1.10.2                                |
| name              | mytest                                   |
| status            | ACTIVE                                   |
| updated           | 2016-01-06T03:10:43                      |
| volume            | 1                                        |
| volume_used       | 0.1                                      |
+-------------------+------------------------------------------+
```

We can see that the instance IP address is **10.1.10.2**. We should be able to ssh to it by using the command:

```
ssh ubuntu@10.1.10.2 -i ~/.ssh/id_rsa
```

ubuntu is the username that we set in the export variable, and the identity file is the private key whose path we exported while creating the image.

 This method only works if we have created the image using the DIB/ Redstack method shown in the previous chapter. If the template was created with any other method, you will have to inject the SSH keys yourself (or create user credentials for the admin user).

```
alokas@DevStack:~$ ssh ubuntu@10.1.10.2 -I ~/.ssh/id_rsa
dlopen /home/alokas/.ssh/id_rsa failed: /home/alokas/.ssh/id_rsa: invalid ELF header
Welcome to Ubuntu 14.04.3 LTS (GNU/Linux 3.13.0-74-generic i686)

 * Documentation:  https://help.ubuntu.com/

  Get cloud support with Ubuntu Advantage Cloud Guest:
    http://www.ubuntu.com/business/services/cloud

Last login: Wed Jan  6 06:11:22 2016 from 10.1.10.1
ubuntu@mytest:~$
```

The guest agent log is located at /var/log/trove/trove-guestagent.log.

As we can see, we are able to log in. You may want to log in in order to troubleshoot if somehow the guest agent doesn't work. You will be able to see the cinder drive mounted with the MySQL data directory pointing to that.

You will also notice that the database engine is installed and started (you can check it with the ps -ef command). If we also take a look at the configuration file, it will be configured based on the configuration template for the particular datastore (more on this in the next chapter).

Launching the instance using the GUI

The GUI is another method that we can use to request ourselves a database instance. More often than not, most of the users will be using this method. So, once we log in to the horizon dashboard, we can go to the **Database** | **Instances** dashboard.

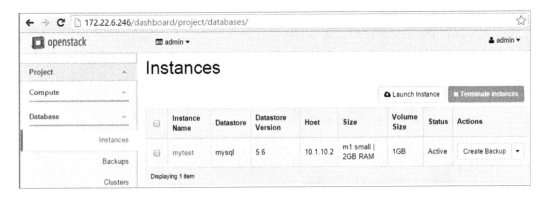

Click on **Create Instance** and we will fill in the details:

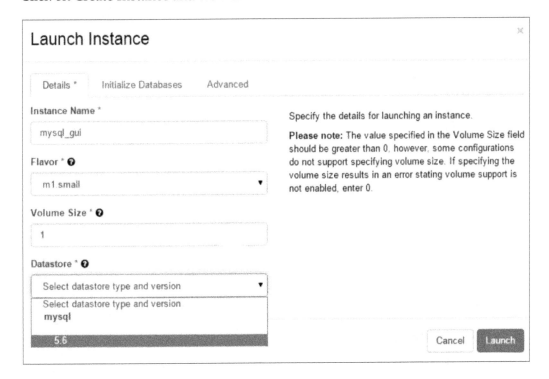

We can also initialize the database and create a database user (we could pass the parameters in the CLI command as well):

We could choose to launch it from a backup image or create a replica, but more on this will be covered in the upcoming chapters:

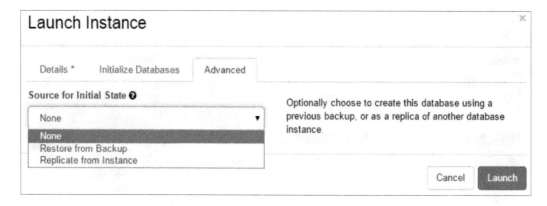

So, we select **None** and then click on **Launch**. The GUI will show the state of the instance. We will wait until the instance is marked **ACTIVE**.

We should be able to access the MySQL database using the username/password over the network.

Connect to the database instance

Now that the instance is created, we can now log in to the database by using the standard MySQL client; we will use the command:

```
mysql -udbuser -pdbpass -h 10.1.10.3
```

```
alokas@DevStack:~$ mysql -udbuser -pdbpass -h 10.1.10.3
Welcome to the MySQL monitor.  Commands end with ; or \g.
Your MySQL connection id is 127
Server version: 5.6.27-0ubuntu0.14.04.1 (Ubuntu)

Copyright (c) 2000, 2015, Oracle and/or its affiliates. All rights reserved.

Oracle is a registered trademark of Oracle Corporation and/or its
affiliates. Other names may be trademarks of their respective
owners.

Type 'help;' or '\h' for help. Type '\c' to clear the current input statement.

mysql> show databases;
+--------------------+
| Database           |
+--------------------+
| information_schema |
| testdb1            |
+--------------------+
2 rows in set (0.02 sec)
```

As we can see, the user is allowed access and access is also granted to **testdb1** that we created.

Instance operations

There are other instance operations that can be performed by Trove.

Resize

We can resize the instance and also the data volume. We can change the volume using the command:

```
trove resize-volume <instance name> <new size>
```

```
trove resize-instance <instance name> <new flavor-id>
```

Example:

```
trove resize-volume mytest 2
```

This will increase the size of the volume to 2 GB. We can execute the instance resize command as well.

We can also perform these operations from the context menu in the GUI using the context menu.

Terminate the Trove instances

If we want to delete the instances that we have created in Trove, the command is:

```
trove delete <instance id>
```

 WARNING: The data on the instance will be deleted irreversibly so we should use it with care. It's a good idea to take a backup of the database before termination.

Let us delete the instance that we created. We will get the instance ID by using the `trove list` command and then execute the `trove delete` command.

```
alokas@DevStack:~$ trove list
+-----------------------------------+----------+-----------+-------------------+
-+------------+--------+
| ID                                | Name     | Datastore | Datastore Version |
| Flavor ID | Size |
+-----------------------------------+----------+-----------+-------------------+
-+------------+--------+
| 813b0155-7740-465d-80f4-cec64e57dae9 | mysql_gui | mysql    | 5.6               |
| 2         | 1    |
| 879dcf19-8fd6-4044-9a4c-30577b5b52dd | mytest   | mysql    | 5.6               |
| 2         | 2    |
+-----------------------------------+----------+-----------+-------------------+
-+------------+--------+
alokas@DevStack:~$ trove delete 879dcf19-8fd6-4044-9a4c-30577b5b52dd
```

The command will delete the instance. This activity can also be done from the context menu in the GUI.

Troubleshooting

If an instance doesn't boot or move to an active state, here are a few steps that you can perform to fix the issues:

1. Check if the Nova instance has booted: This is the first step. Check if the nova instance has successfully changed its state to Running. If not, you may have to troubleshoot the nova system and look at the logs of nova.

2. Guest agent startup: Check that the guest agent is successfully able to start up. You can do this by logging in to the VNC console (if you have set up user credentials) or SSH (if you have set up keys while creating the image).

3. cloud-init: Verify that cloud-init is working as it needs to inject the configuration files for the guest agent.

4. Network between the Trove guest agent and RabbitMQ:

    ◦ Remember that the Trove guest agent needs to connect to the message queue to retrieve its task. If the message is sitting in the `guestagent.<uuid>` queue for a long time and is never acknowledged, then there might be a network issue.

    ◦ Ensure that the `trove-guestagent.conf` configuration file values are correct and that it is pointed to the correct RabbitMQ host with correct credentials.

5. Internet access to the guest instance: If the packages need to be downloaded, ensure that the guest has an available Internet connection. If proxy access needs to be provided, ensure that the local-settings element is used in the DIB.

6. Logs: Check the logs of `trove-api`, `trove-taskmanager`, and finally the guest agents log to troubleshoot the issue.

Summary

In this chapter, we looked at creating instances using the CLI and GUI, connecting to the instance, and also looked at some basic instance operations. Now that we have a functional system, we will take a look at advanced features in the upcoming chapters. In the next chapter, we will look at managing and tuning the databases.

6

Configuring
the Trove Instances

So far, we have successfully installed Trove, created images for the templates, and also spun up instances by using the CLI and the GUI. In this chapter, we will understand the following things about Trove:

- How the default configuration of the instance is determined
- How to make modifications to the configuration of a single or a group of instances using configuration groups in Trove
- How to resize the Trove instances

Default datastore and version configuration

Each database engine, be it MySQL, MongoDB, Percona, and so on, has a default configuration file that the database engine looks for, when starting the service on the guest instance.

The Trove system sends this configuration file using the guest agent (we can see this if we intercept the Prepare message sent in the RabbitMQ queue as shown in the previous chapter). In this section, we will take a look at where Trove stores this information and how we could change it in order to suit our company's needs.

The default configuration that is used by all instances to start up is set in template files. `trove.conf` has a configuration option called `template_path` that is used to specify the folder where the datastore templates are being stored.

The default value of this in a package install is /etc/trove/templates.
On a DevStack instance that we are running, the default value is
trove/templates in the path where Trove is installed. The full path is
/opt/stack/trove/trove/templates.

```
alokas@DevStack:~$ cd /opt/stack/trove/trove/templates/
alokas@DevStack:/opt/stack/trove/trove/templates$ ls
cassandra  couchdb  default.heat.template  mongodb  percona      pxc    vertica
couchbase  db2      mariadb                mysql    postgresql   redis
alokas@DevStack:/opt/stack/trove/trove/templates$
```

This contains one subfolder for each of the datastores that Trove supports.
The templates for a particular datastore are found in the corresponding folder.

So, say if we want to look at the MySQL templates for the configuration, we will
navigate to the mysql folder.

```
alokas@DevStack:/opt/stack/trove/trove/templates$ cd mysql
alokas@DevStack:/opt/stack/trove/trove/templates/mysql$ ls
5.5                      override.config.template         validation-rules.json
config.template   replica.config.template
mysql-test        replica_source.config.template
alokas@DevStack:/opt/stack/trove/trove/templates/mysql$
```

Now that we are in the folder, let us quickly talk about the templating mechanism
that Trove follows. Trove supports templates for every type of configuration
file that it has to create (it has a template for replication, both master and slave
– replica_source.template and replica.template; it also has them for a
single instance configuration – called config.template, and so on.)

All datastores will at least have one configuration template for the single
instance/base configuration (config.template). If there are specific configurations
for a specific datastore version, it is put in a separate folder inside the configuration
template (take a peek inside the 5.5 folder), which is used when that specific
datastore version is instantiated, otherwise the default is used.

If we take a look at the config.template file, we will notice another thing. This
template file is not copied as is. The file is variable based, which is then substituted
before being used by the database engine. The only variable that is used.

If you notice, the configuration values have the flavor['ram'] variable, which is
substituted with the memory size in MB and then the configuration value is set.

```
alokas@DevStack:/opt/stack/trove/trove/templates/mysql$ cat -n config.template
     1  [client]
     2  port = 3306
     3
     4  [mysqld_safe]
     5  nice = 0
     6
     7  [mysqld]
     8  user = mysql
     9  port = 3306
    10  basedir = /usr
    11  datadir = /var/lib/mysql/data
    12  ####tmpdir = /tmp
    13  tmpdir = /var/tmp
    14  pid_file = /var/run/mysqld/mysqld.pid
    15  skip-external-locking = 1
    16  key_buffer_size = {{ (50 * flavor['ram']/512)|int }}M
    17  max_allowed_packet = {{ (1024 * flavor['ram']/512)|int }}K
    18  thread_stack = 192K
........
........
    55
    56  !includedir /etc/mysql/conf.d/
alokas@DevStack:/opt/stack/trove/trove/templates/mysql$
```

For example, key_buffer_size will be set to 200 M (50 * 2048 / 512) for an
m1.small (2048 MB RAM) and 400 M for an m1.medium instance. (In order to see the
RAM size for the instances, use the command trove flavor-list.)

> We can modify the template file by editing it using your favorite
> text editor. The change made takes effect immediately and the new
> template is used on the next instance of the datastore that Trove
> creates after the modification.

One other thing that is found in the folder is validation-rules.json. This file,
as its name suggests, performs validation on the user-defined configuration groups
(which we will see in the next section of the chapter).

As Trove administrators, we can modify the `validation-rules.json` file, in order to add/remove configuration capability and to set the minimum and the maximum allowed values. As an example, looking at the `sort_buffer_size` configuration from the default `validation-rules` file:

```
{
    "name": "sort_buffer_size",
    "restart_required": false,
    "max": 18446744073709551615,
    "min": 32768,
    "type": "integer"
},
```

If our standard dictates that the minimum value for this configuration parameter should be 65536, we should be able to modify the file and load this using the command `trove-manage db_load_datastore_config_parameters`. The full syntax and the command in action can be seen in the later part of the chapter.

Now that we know about the template file, if we need to know the values that have been computed (based on the formulas) and passed along for a particular instance, we can see the default configuration of an instance by typing the command `trove configuration-default <instance name>`. In the following screenshot, we take a look at the configuration of our instance `mysql_gui`, which is an `m1.small`:

```
alokas@DevStack:~$ trove configuration-default mysql_gui
+-------------------------+---------------------------+
| Property                | Value                     |
+-------------------------+---------------------------+
| basedir                 | /usr                      |
| connect_timeout         | 15                        |
| datadir                 | /var/lib/mysql/data       |
| default_storage_engine  | innodb                    |
| innodb_buffer_pool_size | 600M                      |
| innodb_data_file_path   | ibdata1:10M:autoextend    |
| innodb_file_per_table   | 1                         |
| innodb_log_buffer_size  | 25M                       |
| innodb_log_file_size    | 50M                       |
| innodb_log_files_in_group | 2                       |
| join_buffer_size        | 1M                        |
| key_buffer_size         | 200M                      |
| local-infile            | 0                         |
| max_allowed_packet      | 4096K                     |
| max_connections         | 400                       |
| max_heap_table_size     | 64M                       |
| max_user_connections    | 400                       |
| myisam-recover          | BACKUP                    |
| open_files_limit        | 2048                      |
| performance_schema      | ON                        |
| pid_file                | /var/run/mysqld/mysqld.pid |
| port                    | 3306                      |
| query_cache_limit       | 1M                        |
| query_cache_size        | 32M                       |
| query_cache_type        | 1                         |
```

The command format might lead us to believe that these are the default values running on the instance itself. However, these are simply from the `config.template` file after substitution. If the template has been modified after the instance was instantiated, these values will be wrong. In a production environment, it is recommended that we design the default configuration file for a particular datastore version before the system goes live and after that all configuration modifications can be done by modifying the default configuration.

Modifying the default configuration file is as easy as editing the `config.template` file. For instance, if we want `innodb_log_file_size` to be 100 M rather than the default 50 MB, we will simply edit the `config.template` file in the templates directory and make the change.

Do note that this configuration doesn't get updated in the instances that have already been requested using the older configuration template. (but when you look at the `trove configuration-default` command output, you might be led to believe erroneously that the older systems have also been updated. Hence, it is recommended to modify the default configuration before setting the datastore in production)

In order to test this, let us request another MySQL instance called `test12` using our `trove create` command:

```
alokas@DevStack:~$ trove show test12
+-------------------+------------------------------------------+
| Property          | Value                                    |
+-------------------+------------------------------------------+
| created           | 2016-02-26T15:48:00                      |
| datastore         | mysql                                    |
| datastore_version | 5.6                                      |
| flavor            | 2                                        |
| id                | 8b4a3784-f9c1-471d-8fbf-7995e250385a     |
| ip                | 10.1.10.3                                |
| name              | test12                                   |
| status            | ACTIVE                                   |
| updated           | 2016-02-26T15:48:26                      |
| volume            | 1                                        |
+-------------------+------------------------------------------+
```

The instance is created with the same specs as that of our older `mysql_gui` instance that we created.

We will run remote `ssh` commands to verify that it is indeed the case (`10.1.10.2` is the old `mysql_gui` instance and `10.1.10.3` is the newer `test12` instance).

It is absolutely not necessary to SSH into a Trove instance. This is only to show that the configuration file has been modified on one instance and not on the other.

```
alokas@DevStack:~$ ssh -i ~/.ssh/id_rsa ubuntu@10.1.10.3 'cat /etc/mysql/my.cnf' | grep innodb_log_file_size
innodb_log_file_size=100M
alokas@DevStack:~$
alokas@DevStack:~$ ssh -i ~/.ssh/id_rsa ubuntu@10.1.10.2 'cat /etc/mysql/my.cnf' | grep innodb_log_file_size
innodb_log_file_size=50M
```

As we can see, the configuration of the old instance is not changed but the new instance has the new log file size.

Modifying the instance configuration

So, we have seen how the default configuration can be modified. But what about the instances that are already available and running? Can we make configuration changes to those? The answer to this question is very much a yes.

Configuration groups

Let us look at the Trove configuration groups. These technically are some configurations that can be applied on one or more instances. It is to be noted that at any given point in time, only one configuration group can be active.

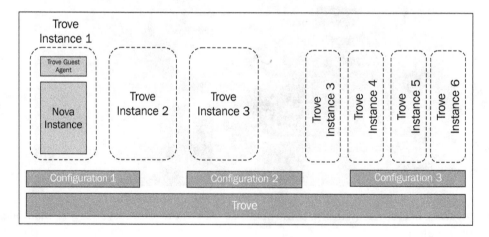

The steps in using the configuration groups are:

1. Define the modifiable configuration parameters (in the
    `validation-rules.json` file): A copy of validation-rules is
    provided by default; we can modify it as needed.

2. Upload the configuration parameters in the Trove system: This is a one-time
    activity that is done when `validation-rules.json` is changed.

3. Create a configuration.

4. Attach it to one or more instances.

The configuration is synchronized across the instances. This means that, once the
configuration is created and attached, modifying the configuration will modify it
on all the instances that it is associated with. This makes it extremely useful when
we want different configurations for different groups of instances (think about the
configuration of prod/dev).

Defining configuration parameters

Trove already ships with a `validation-rules.json` file in its templates directory
(the same directory where we found the base configuration template).

Each parameter will have the following properties (please note that this is a JSON
string and hence the curly braces are delimiters):

```
3        {
4               "name": "innodb_file_per_table",
5               "restart_required": false,
6               "max": 1,
7               "min": 0,
8               "type": "integer"
9        },
```

There are several of these and you can see that the instructions for the configuration
and whether the instance needs to be rebooted are mentioned in the JSON file. This
file, with its default values, is more than enough for most cases, but we could modify
the parameter values in certain cases (for example, `innodb_log_buffer_size`,
where we can tweak the min/max value as per your standards). This is merely
defining configuration parameters in a file and these values do not take effect
until the next step is completed.

Uploading configuration parameters

We can check the configuration parameters that are currently defined by using the command `trove configuration-parameter-list --datastore <Datastore name> <datstore version>`, so we will execute.

`trove configuration-parameter-list --datastore mysql 5.6`

```
alokas@DevStack:~$ trove configuration-parameter-list --datastore mysql 5.6
+--------+--------+----------+----------+------------------+
| Name   | Type   | Min Size | Max Size | Restart Required |
+--------+--------+----------+----------+------------------+
+--------+--------+----------+----------+------------------+
```

This is expected as we have not loaded `validation-rules.json` yet.

If we try attaching a configuration to a datastore, whose configuration parameters have not been initialized, we will get an error stating that the configuration groups is not supported for that particular datastore.

Now, we will upload the `validation-rules.json` file by using the command `trove-manage db_load_datastore_config_parameters mysql 5.6 \`

`/opt/stack/trove/trove/templates/mysql/validation-rules.json`

The `db_load_datastore_config_parameters` command takes the datastore name, datastore version, and file path as inputs and uploads the configuration template. Once the command succeeds, we can execute the parameter list one more time and we shall see the following output:

```
alokas@DevStack:~$ trove configuration-parameter-list --datastore mysql 5.6
+---------------------------+---------+----------+----------+------------------+
| Name                      | Type    | Min Size | Max Size | Restart Required |
+---------------------------+---------+----------+----------+------------------+
| auto_increment_increment  | integer |          |          |            False |
| auto_increment_offset     | integer |          |          |            False |
| autocommit                | integer |          |          |            False |
| bulk_insert_buffer_size   | integer |          |          |            False |
| character_set_client      | string  |          |          |            False |
| character_set_connection  | string  |          |          |            False |
| character_set_database    | string  |          |          |            False |
| character_set_filesystem  | string  |          |          |            False |
```

Now, we can move on to the next step.

Creating a configuration

Now, we need to create a configuration patch that we need to apply to an instance or a group of instances. This is done by using the `configuration-create` command.

The command takes the configuration parameters as a JSON string (key-value pair) and separated by commas.

```
trove configuration-create test-configuration \
    --datastore mysql --datastore_version 5.6 \
    '{ "max_connections":200, "max_user_connections":200 }' \
    --description "Testing Configuration Group"
```

```
alokas@DevStack:~$ trove configuration-create test-configuration \
>    --datastore mysql --datastore_version 5.6 \
>    '{ "max_connections":200, "max_user_connections":200 }' \
>    --description "Testing Configuration Group"
+-----------------------+-----------------------------------------------------+
| Property              | Value                                               |
+-----------------------+-----------------------------------------------------+
| created               | 2016-01-14T01:42:15                                 |
| datastore_name        | mysql                                               |
| datastore_version_id  | 664c7068-e55b-4ddf-bad1-8e65b7798799                |
| datastore_version_name| 5.6                                                 |
| description           | Testing Configuration Group                         |
| id                    | 26a1d629-df68-42bc-826b-684af8f70e64                |
| instance_count        | 0                                                   |
| name                  | test-configuration                                  |
| updated               | 2016-01-14T01:42:15                                 |
| values                | {u'max_user_connections': 200, u'max_connections': 200} |
+-----------------------+-----------------------------------------------------+
```

The previous output shows the configuration that was created. We can now apply this configuration to the instance of our choice.

Applying the configuration to an instance

We can apply the configuration by using the `configuration-attach` command, which has the format `trove configuration-attach <instance name / id> <configuration id>`; we will use the instance `mysql_gui` and the ID of test-configuration.

```
trove configuration-attach mysql_gui 26a1d629-df68-42bc-826b-684af8f70e64
```

This command provides no output if successful, but we would have applied our recently created configuration to the `mysql_gui` instance. We can apply the configuration to as many instances of the same datastore type and version as we please.

We can also use `trove update <instance_name> --configuration <config id>` in order to attach the configuration to the instance.

If the configuration needs a restart, the changes will not be effective immediately and we will see the status **RESTART_REQUIRED** in the `trove list` command.

We can choose to apply the configuration and restart the instance later, by using the command `trove restart <instance_id / name>`. In our case, this will be

`trove restart mysql_gui.`

This will restart the MySQL instance and disconnect any active connections to the system. It is recommended that this be done only during the change window for a production instance.

Verification

In order to verify that the configuration has indeed been applied, we can log in to the instance using the MySQL command line.

`mysql -udbuser -pdbpass -h 10.1.10.2`

Once logged in, execute the following command:

`show global variables like '%max_connections%';`

```
mysql> show global variables like '%max_connections%';
+-----------------+-------+
| Variable_name   | Value |
+-----------------+-------+
| max_connections | 200   |
+-----------------+-------+
```

This should show that the max connections have been set to **200** from the default 400. We can also use the command format `select @@global.<variable name>`.

```
mysql> select @@global.max_user_connections;
+-------------------------------+
| @@global.max_user_connections |
+-------------------------------+
|                           200 |
+-------------------------------+
1 row in set (0.01 sec)
```

The `override.config.template` file from the `templates` folder is used for creating the overridden configuration file and is placed in the `mysql/conf.d` folder on the instance.

 The file can be seen on the instance only after logging in to the instance using SSH or VNC Console. This is not a required step; however, for the purposes of understanding the working, we may want to do it.

A screenshot showing the overridden `config` file is shown on the instance.

```
ubuntu@mysql-gui:/etc/mysql/conf.d$ ls
20-user-001-common.cnf     mysqld_safe_syslog.cnf
50-system-001-common.cnf   no_perf_schema.cnf
ubuntu@mysql-gui:/etc/mysql/conf.d$
ubuntu@mysql-gui:/etc/mysql/conf.d$ cat 20-user-001-common.cnf
[mysqld]
max_user_connections = 200
max_connections = 200
```

Hence, the configuration on an instance is persisted across instance reboots.

Viewing the configuration

If we want to check the contents of the configuration, we will use the `trove configuration-show` command with the configuration ID, which can be retrieved by the `trove configuration-list` command.

So, in our case, we will execute the `trove configuration-list` command and note down the ID for the configuration we are trying to retrieve (in our case, **26a1d629-df68-42bc-826b-684af8f70e64**).

```
alokas@DevStack:/opt/stack/trove/trove/common$ trove configuration-list
+--------------------------------------+------------------+--------------------------------+
------------------+
| ID                                   | Name             | Description                    |
rsion Name |
+--------------------------------------+------------------+--------------------------------+
------------------+
| 26a1d629-df68-42bc-826b-684af8f70e64 | test-configuration | Testing Configuration Group |
                 |
| 7765f929-d617-4d0a-b057-009c7060eb63 | port-change      | Changing Port                  |
                 |
+--------------------------------------+------------------+--------------------------------+
```

We will then execute the `trove configuration-show 26a1d629-df68-42bc-826b-684af8f70e64` command to see the values.

```
+-----------------------+--------------------------------------------------------+
| Property              | Value                                                  |
+-----------------------+--------------------------------------------------------+
| created               | 2016-01-14T01:42:15                                    |
| datastore_name        | mysql                                                  |
| datastore_version_name | 5.6                                                   |
| description           | Testing Configuration Group                            |
| id                    | 26a1d629-df68-42bc-826b-684af8f70e64                   |
| instance_count        | 1                                                      |
| name                  | test-configuration                                     |
| updated               | 2016-01-14T01:42:15                                    |
| values                | {"max_user_connections": 200, "max_connections": 200} |
+-----------------------+--------------------------------------------------------+
```

As we can see, the configuration sets **max_user_connections** and **max_connections** to a certain value.

In order to check which instances are associated with this configuration, we will execute `trove configuration-instances <configuration id>`.

```
+--------------------------------------+-----------+
| ID                                   | Name      |
+--------------------------------------+-----------+
| 1c85ded7-2e6d-4f96-9740-5b25380ec2ea | mysql_gui |
+--------------------------------------+-----------+
```

This shows that the configuration is only applied to a single instance (`mysql_gui`) at the moment.

Patching the configuration

Once the configuration is applied to an instance or a bunch of instances, we can patch the configuration and it will be applied to all the instances attached to the configuration.

In order to effectively understand the use of patching, we will also attach the configuration to our second guest instance (`test12`) using the command `trove configuration-attach test12 26a1d629-df68-42bc-826b-684af8f70e64`. If you don't already have a second instance, you can launch it.

Once this is done, we can ensure that both instances show up in the output of the `trove configuration-instances` command output.

The patching of the configuration is done by using the command format:

```
trove configuration-patch <configuration-id> <JSON for the patch>.
```

In our case, we will drop `max_user_connections` to `150` rather than 300:

```
trove configuration-patch 26a1d629-df68-42bc-826b-684af8f70e64 \
'{ "max_user_connections": 150 }'
```

We can verify that the configuration was patched by looking at the output of the `trove configuration-show <configuration-id>` command. We can also verify by using a similar method that we used to verify in the *Applying configuration* section: `mysql -udbuser -pdbpass -h 10.1.10.2 \`.

```
-e "select @@global.max_user_connections;"
```

This should give you an output of 150, rather than the previous 200.

We should be able to create a new database user and password for the second instance as we did not specify it during the create time.

```
trove database-create test12 testdb2
trove user-create test12 dbuser2 dbpass2
trove user-grant-access test12 dbuser2 testdb2
```

The preceding creates a database (`testdb2`) and user (`dbuser2`) with the password (`dbpass2`) and grants access to the newly created database. Check on the second instance (`Test12`) `mysql -udbuser2 -pdbpass2 -h10.1.10.3 \`

```
-e "select @@global.max_user_connections;"
```

We will notice that this also has the same configuration.

```
+------------------------------------+
| @@global.max_user_connections |
+------------------------------------+
|                          150 |
+------------------------------------+
```

If you remember, we had changed the default configuration port to 3307 before spinning the test12 instance; hence, the port needs to be specified.

Updating the configuration

The difference between patching and updating is that the update command should replace the entire contents of the configuration and not just update the values in the configuration. The command format is as following:

```
trove configuration-update <config id> '<new JSON>'
```

> At the time of writing this book, there is a documented bug (Bug ID: 1449238), https://bugs.launchpad.net/trove/+bug/1449238, which doesn't completely replace it but leaves the old configuration in.
>
> Say we want to replace test-configuration with just setting wait_timeout to 300 (the default is set to 120 – check the configuration-default output), we will use the command.

```
trove configuration-update 26a1d629-df68-42bc-826b-684af8f70e64 \
'{ "wait_timeout": 300 }'
```

We verify it with the trove configuration-show command.

```
+-----------------------+--------------------------------------------+
| Property              | Value                                      |
+-----------------------+--------------------------------------------+
| created               | 2016-01-14T01:42:15                        |
| datastore_name        | mysql                                      |
| datastore_version_name| 5.6                                        |
| description           | Testing Configuration Group                |
| id                    | 26a1d629-df68-42bc-826b-684af8f70e64       |
| instance_count        | 2                                          |
| name                  | test-configuration                         |
| updated               | 2016-01-14T08:26:49                        |
| values                | {"wait_timeout": 300}                      |
+-----------------------+--------------------------------------------+
```

This will update the configuration; however, please remember that due to the bug, even the older configuration will still exist.

```
ubuntu@mysql-gui:/etc/mysql/conf.d$ cat 20-user-001-common.cnf
[mysqld]
wait_timeout = 300
max_user_connections = 150
max_connections = 200
```

This is effectively the bug; once the bug resolves, this will not exist.

In order to ensure that this doesn't happen, we should detach the configuration and reattach it, so that the older configuration doesn't exist.

Removing the configuration

The configuration can be removed from the two instance commands:

- `trove update <instance_name> --remove_configuration`
- `trove configuration-detach <instance_name>`

This restores the configuration to the default configuration. Please note that this is the configuration in `my.cnf` (which was generated from the default configuration when the instance was spun up and may be different from the current default configuration).

```
alokas@DevStack:~$ trove configuration-detach mysql_gui
alokas@DevStack:~$
```

This command, as you can see, has no output.

If a restart is required for the service, you need to execute `trove restart <instance name/id>` before you can reapply a new configuration.

Verification

We can execute the same commands that we did to verify that the configuration took effect. We will also see that the file has been removed from the guest instance.

```
ubuntu@mysql-gui:/etc/mysql/conf.d$ ls
50-system-001-common.cnf  mysqld_safe_syslog.cnf  no_perf_schema.cnf
ubuntu@mysql-gui:/etc/mysql/conf.d$
```

Please notice that the `20-user-001-common.cnf` file no longer exists.

Adding a new parameter

We can only add the configuration parameters that are listed in the output of the `trove configuration-parameter-list` command. This is populated from the `validation-rules.json` file that we imported earlier.

Let's take a use case: in a company X, in the dev/test environment, the MySQL database instances run on port 3308 and production instances run on the default port 3306, but port is not a valid configuration parameter and if we try to create a configuration, we will get an error like **ERROR: The configuration parameter port is not supported for this datastore: MySQL 5.6. (HTTP 422.)**. We will need to modify `validation-rules.json`. So in this case, we will add the JSON (I have added somewhere in between. There is no dependency on the placement of this).

```
 94            {
 95                    "name": "port",
 96                    "restart_required": true,
 97                    "max": 65535,
 98                    "min": 1025,
 99                    "type": "integer"
100            },
```

So, the configuration is `port`, which is an integer value and can be from `1025` to `65535` as they are non-privileged ports. We will need to restart the MySQL instance when we are changing the port, so `restart_required` is set to `true`.

Once the `validation-rules.json` file is modified, we will upload it using `trove-manage db_load_datastore_config_parameters` and then follow the process from creating a configuration and applying it.

Modifying the port is not supported by Trove; however, it can be performed as shown earlier. If we have to modify the port, please remember to change the port for the network security group or the database will be inaccessible. Different datastores may have different configuration strategies, but most of them implement the default file configuration. The databases that allow configuration management during the time of writing are MySQL, MariaDB, Percona, Percona XtraDB, and Redis. Other database support for configuration changes is planned in the near future.

Summary

In this chapter, we have basically looked at configuring and tuning databases. Some of the key tasks include defining configuration groups, defining configuration parameters, patching and updating the configuration, defining and uploading configuration parameters, and finally adding a new parameter.

In the next chapter, we shall look at the most common DBA task, which is backup management of the databases.

7
Database Backup and Restore

Data being critical in every enterprise IT, it needs to be protected. This protection is done at various levels, by creating a cluster/replica to ensure more than one hot/warm copy of the data exists.

In order to have a cold copy of the data for disaster recovery, a database backup is normally taken. Database backups and restore are possibly one of the most important operational tasks of a DBA. Trove helps automate the entire process, from backing it up, encrypting data at rest, and also restoring the backup. Trove also supports incremental backups of your databases and supports creating a new instance from an existing backup.

In this chapter, we will cover the following topics:

- Formulating a backup and recovery plan
- The concept of strategies in Trove
- Configuration aspects
- Backing up and restoring Trove guest instances

Formulating a backup and recovery plan

There are two kinds of backups: full backup and incremental backup. Trove helps with both of the backups (with certain data stores), as we will see later in the chapter. A plan needs to be formulated in order to successfully execute these.

The frequency of both or either of these backups needs to be based on the following parameters:

- Importance of the data
- Frequency of changes in the database
- Recovery objectives (RTO, RPO)

Based on the preceding parameters, we will need to derive the following key points:

- Frequency of full backups
- Frequency of incremental backups (if any)
- Frequency of testing the backups (by restoring the database)
- Need for offsite shipping of the database backup
- Frequency and modes of offsite shipping

This plan is applicable to any form of backup and this will help us with scripting and automating the backup tasks.

Backing up/restoring in Trove

Trove uses backup strategies in order to back up the database. The backups are stored as defined in the storage strategy (defaults to Swift), which is at object storage system. The backup is encrypted by default to protect the data in rest.

There can be several use cases of backup and restore in Trove:

- Cold copy of data for recovery purposes
- Point in time snapshot in order to create a different branch of development
- Multiple copies of the database independent of each other for purposes like auditing, running reports based on old data, and so on

The Trove system internally uses backup and restore strategies to seed the replication data (discussed in the next chapter). Let's now dive in and see how the backup/restore methodology works in Trove.

The concept of strategies in Trove

Strategy in the world of Trove means a construct that allows developers to extend the functionalities of Trove by writing specialized implementations that can be abstracted.

This is a fully pluggable architecture, and what this actually means is that different technologies and different codes can be used to perform the same functions across different database engines.

The concept of strategies is used for backups, restores, replication, clustering, and storage (this determines where the backups are stored along with its associated properties). These are implemented in the guest agent code (can also be implemented for the API and task manager components), which also makes the code run closest to the place where the action has to happen.

So, effectively, each strategy needs to implement a list of functions at a minimum (these can be seen in the base.py file for that particular strategy), which the system can then use to call and perform the functions.

For example, each backup strategy needs to provide a command that needs to be executed in order to take the backup, and each storage strategy needs to implement a save function, which will allow us to save to that particular storage system.

The following diagram shows the concept of strategies. It also shows that the control components use an abstracted term and send the message using the message bus, say **create_backup**, and the guest agent looks at the default or configured strategy for that particular database engine and executes those commands.

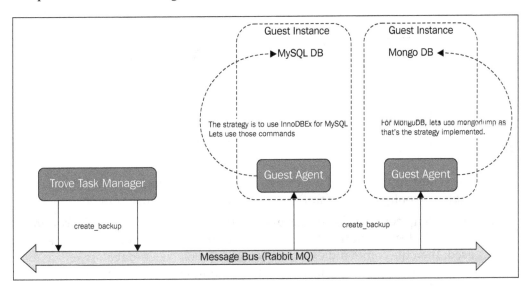

The concept is valid for everything that supports the strategies. Please note that not all the control components are shown in this case and the diagram is for representation purposes only.

The backup/restore strategy in action

In order to better understand how the strategy will work, let's take a look at the following diagram that shows the backup taking place. The steps are enumerated as follows:

1. The **Trove API** passes on the command to the **Trove Task Manager**.

2. The **Trove Task Manager** leaves a **Message** in the **Rabbit MQ** queue for the **Guest Agent** to pick up.

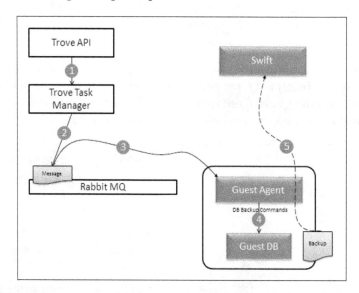

3. The **Guest Agent** pulls the message and checks the backup and storage strategy (configured/default) for the particular data store version.

4. The backup commands are executed by the guest agent. (It gets the command by the strategy definition.) For example, if the MySQLDump strategy is used, then the command executed is `mysqldump --all-databases -user <username> --password`, along with the command to zip and encrypt the backup (these are all defined in the strategy files (as shown in the next section)).

5. The **Guest Agent** stores the backup as stored in the storage strategy.

Configuring the backup strategies

The strategies are configured by default, but we can choose to override them. The configuration options are:

- `backup_strategy`: The name of the strategy to use, for example, InnoBackupEx, MySQLDump, MongoDump, and so on

- `backup_namespace`: The file to load the code for the strategies from

- `backup_incremental_strategy`: The name of the strategy that needs to be used while taking incremental backups

These configuration options are set in the `trove-guestagent.conf` file, which will inject them to the guest during build time.

We don't have to configure anything additional in the guest agent configuration; this section is purely informational.

In order to understand the different strategies available to us and the corresponding namespaces, let us take a look at the following table, which shows the different backup strategies that are available in Trove at the time of writing the book:

Data store name / Backup type	Strategy name	Strategy namespace
MySQL / Full	MySQLDump	`trove.guestagent.strategies.backup.mysql_impl`
MySQL / Full	InnoBackupEX	`trove.guestagent.strategies.backup.mysql_impl`
MySOL / Incremental	InnoBackupExIncremental	`trove.guestagent.strategies.backup.mysql_impl`
Couchbase / Full	CbBackup	`trove.guestagent.strategies.backup.experimental.couchbase_impl`
Mongo DB / Full	MongoDump	`trove.guestagent.strategies.backup.experimental.mongo_impl`
PostgreSQL / Full	PgDump	`trove.guestagent.strategies.backup.experimental.postgresql_imp`
Redis / Full	RedisBackup	`trove.guestagent.strategies.backup.expreimental.redis_impl`

As we can see, at this point in time, only MySQL (and its variants like MariaDB) have the ability to perform the incremental backup and offer two strategies for full backup (if we choose not to use InnoDB, we could just use MySQLDump). Also, not all the different data stores support full backup at this moment.

This means that we can also implement a simple backup strategy of our choice, if we so choose, by writing a different Python class. However, in most cases, we don't have to as the ones provided by default with Trove are sufficient.

Configuring the storage strategies

The storage strategy denotes the place where the backups can be stored. At the time of writing this book, only SwiftStorage, which is the object storage in OpenStack, has been implemented. The default configuration parameters are:

- `storage_strategy`: The name of the storage strategy
- `storage_namespace`: The file where this strategy is implemented

There are plans to add support for other storage strategies like AWS S3 and so on. But since this is the only strategy available to us at the moment, let us take a moment to also look at its sub-configuration parameters. The bucket, where the backups need to be stored, whether the backup needs to be encrypted, if it needs to be encrypted, what key needs to be used, and so on. All of these are configured using the following configuration variables:

- `backup_swift_container`: The place where the backups will be stored (default value is `database_backups`)
- `backup_use_gzip_compression`: Do we compress the backup (default is `true`)
- `backup_use_openssl_encryption`: Do we encrypt the backup (default is `true`)
- `backup_aes_cbc_key`: Which key to use for encryption
- `backup_use_snet`: Can the backup use the Swift service network (default is `false`)
- `backup_chunk_size`: Chunk size for backups
- `backup_segment_max_size`: Max size for each segment of the backup

Most times, the default would work fine. But these options can be configured should we need to tweak their values.

Backup prerequisites

The requisites for backup are fairly simple:

- We have a database for which backup has to be taken.
- The Swift system is configured and accessible. (In DevStack, please check if the Swift services are enabled.)
- There is space in the Swift system to store backups.
- All required configuration options are in place.

In our case, we don't have to worry about the last point as we will leave the entire configuration to the default values. Also, we have the second and third point taken care of. Since we are using MySQL as the database, the first point also has been satisfied. (Please note that while creating the DIB image, we installed the InnoDB tool by using the ubuntu-mysql element provided. So, we are good to go.)

Backups and restores

Now that we have established that the prerequisites are in order, we will perform the actual functions.

Full backup

The Trove command line with the backup-create option helps us create a full backup of the database.

Please note that backup/restore may turn off (or pause) the database service for a brief moment to ensure that data is not corrupted. So, caution should be exercised while taking backups or performing restores of production databases.

The command format is trove backup-create <instance-id> <backup-name>. Please remember that we can check the instance ID using the trove list command.

So, in order to back up the test12 database, we would execute:

```
trove backup-create 723c048e-bd5b-4e1a-84cd-836be970d7db myfirstbackup-1
```

```
+-------------+----------------------------------------------------
| Property    | Value
+-------------+----------------------------------------------------
| created     | 2016-01-23T21:48:43
| datastore   | {u'version': u'5.6', u'type': u'mysql', u'version_id':
| description | None
| id          | e3737982-2220-42a3-8e63-52d61f73f523
| instance_id | 723c048e-bd5b-4e1a-84cd-836be970d7db
| locationRef | None
| name        | myfirstbackup
| parent_id   | None
| size        | None
| status      | NEW
| updated     | 2016-01-23T21:48:43
+-------------+----------------------------------------------------
```

The details of the backup are shown on the screen. The backup command also backs up the metadata, which is especially useful while restoring or creating another database from the current backup.

Incremental backup

Incremental backup, as we know, is only supported for MySQL at this time, and we can perform an incremental backup of the database that we just backed up.

For the incremental backup to work, we will obviously need a parent or a full backup to anchor the incremental backup onto, so we will need the backup-id of a full backup to be used as a parent.

We will use the last backup we just took, whose id was e3737982-2220-42a3-8e63-52d61f73f523 (it will be different for you).

The command format to take the incremental backup is similar to that of the full backup. The only exception is that a --parent parameter is being passed, so it will be trove backup-create <instance-id> <backup name> --parent <parent backup-id>.

So, we will execute the following command:

```
trove backup-create 723c048e-bd5b-4e1a-84cd-836be970d7db incremental-bkp
--parent e3737982-2220-42a3-8e63-52d61f73f523
```

```
+---------------+---------------------------------------------+
| Property      | Value                                       |
+---------------+---------------------------------------------+
| created       | 2016-01-23T21:59:49                         |
| datastore     | {u'version': u'5.6', u'type': u'mysql',     |
| description   | None                                        |
| id            | e8ba6800-7ff0-40c8-9dd3-e396b84dd4f1        |
| instance_id   | 723c048e-bd5b-4e1a-84cd-836be970d7db        |
| locationRef   | None                                        |
| name          | incremental-bkp                             |
| parent_id     | e3737982-2220-42a3-8e63-52d61f73f523        |
| size          | None                                        |
| status        | NEW                                         |
| updated       | 2016-01-23T21:59:49                         |
+---------------+---------------------------------------------+
```

The output is similar, with the exception of **parent_id** being shown.

Viewing the backup

The backups can be listed by using the `trove backup-list` command:

trove backup-list

```
+-------------+------------------+-----------------+-----------+------------------+-----------------------+
| ID          | Instance ID      | Name            | Status    | Parent ID        | Updated               |
+-------------+------------------+-----------------+-----------+------------------+-----------------------+
| e3737982-...| 723c048e-bd5b-...| myfirstbackup   | COMPLETED | None             | 2016-01-23T21:49:58   |
| e8ba6800-...| 723c048e-bd5b-...| incremental-bkp | COMPLETED | e3737982-2220-...| 2016-01-23T22:00:56   |
+-------------+------------------+-----------------+-----------+------------------+-----------------------+
```

The output shows that **incremental-bkp** has **myfirstbackup** as its parent. The backup is also stored in the Swift storage, so let us take a look at the Swift containers, by using the command `swift list`.

```
alokas@DevStack:~$ swift list
database_backups
```

As we can see, only the `database_backups` container is created. Please note that this is a default name for the Swift container and can be overridden by the configuration variables as shown in the previous sections.

If you get a user warning that states **UserWarning: Providing attr without filter_value to get_urls() is deprecated as of the 1.7.0 release** while executing the Swift command, you will need to set an additional environmental variable called `OS_REGION_NAME`.

Please set this to the default region name of your system. You can view this by executing the command `keystone endpoint-list` and then looking under the region. For us, it was `RegionOne`, so we export the variable with the following command:

export OS_REGION_NAME=RegionOne

We will then look into the container itself, by typing the command:

swift list database_backups

```
alokas@DevStack:~$ swift list database_backups
e3737982-2220-42a3-8e63-52d61f73f523.xbstream.gz.enc
e3737982-2220-42a3-8e63-52d61f73f523_00000000
e8ba6800-7ff0-40c8-9dd3-e396b84dd4f1.xbstream.gz.enc
e8ba6800-7ff0-40c8-9dd3-e396b84dd4f1_00000000
```

While we could technically download these backups elsewhere, please remember that these backups are encrypted (by default) and will be of no use outside Trove, unless the key is known.

Restoring backups

In Trove, the restoration of the database is not done directly, but by creating a new instance and loading the data onto it. We can restore from a full backup or an incremental backup. If we choose to restore from an incremental backup, the entire chain (up to the last parent full backup) is restored onto the system.

So, in order to create a new instance from a backup, we simply use the `trove create` command passing `-backup` parameter, `trove create <name> <flavor-id> --size <volume size> --backup <backup-id>`.

In our case, we will use incremental backup to ensure the full chain restore happens.

```
trove create copyoftest 2 --size 1 \
--backup e8ba6800-7ff0-40c8-9dd3-e396b84dd4f1 \
--datastore mysql --datastore_version 5.6
```

```
+----------------------+-------------------------------------------+
| Property             | Value                                     |
+----------------------+-------------------------------------------+
| created              | 2016-01-23T22:42:28                       |
| datastore            | mysql                                     |
| datastore_version    | 5.6                                       |
| flavor               | 2                                         |
| id                   | 095792f9-1763-432b-b738-716da30134c3      |
| name                 | copyoftest                                |
| status               | BUILD                                     |
| updated              | 2016-01-23T22:42:28                       |
| volume               | 1                                         |
+----------------------+-------------------------------------------+
```

The new instance starts building and once it gets to the active state, we can verify that the same databases were found.

Deleting backups

The backup can be deleted by the `trove backup-delete` command by passing `backup-id` as the argument to the command. It is to be noted that we should only delete the full backups after all the incremental backups dependent on them are deleted. If the parent is deleted, then Trove automatically deletes the dependent backups as well.

So, here we delete the parent backup:

```
trove backup-delete e3737982-2220-42a3-8e63-52d61f73f523
```

When we execute a subsequent `backup-list`, we see that both the backups were deleted, as the incremental backup was dependent on the parent.

```
alokas@DevStack:/opt/stack/logs$ trove backup-list
+------+--------------+--------+----------+------------+----------+
| ID   | Instance ID  | Name   | Status   | Parent ID  | Updated  |
+------+--------------+--------+----------+------------+----------+
+------+--------------+--------+----------+------------+----------+
```

Summary

In this chapter, we dealt with backups and restores of the database. We have learned about the ways backup is implemented in Trove. In the next and final chapter, we will look at more advanced features such as replication and clustering.

8
Advanced Database Features

We are at the last leg of our journey and so far we have seen how Trove can help users in creating, configuring, resizing, taking backups, and restoring different data stores. However, all of these tasks deal with a single instance.

With something as important as data (especially if it is production data), no organization in the world will risk running a single instance. Therefore, in a production setup, it is imperative that some sort of high availability for databases is introduced.

While there are several options, two of the most used ones are replication and clustering when it comes to databases.

In this chapter, we will deal with these features of Trove. Currently, these features are only available for some of the databases that Trove supports.

Another point to keep in mind is that Trove itself is not the provider for these features, but merely provides a platform to help configure these if the underlying databases themselves support it. Which means if database engine type X doesn't support a feature (replication or clustering), then Trove cannot be used to set that up.

Trove enables these features using strategies (the same concept that was seen in the previous chapter for backups).

In this chapter, we will go over the following topics:

- Understanding replication and clustering
- How to set up replication in Trove and the different failover options available to the administrator
- How to set up clustering in Trove

The replication example will be set up in the MySQL data store and we already have the image created for MySQL. For the clustering piece, we will use MongoDB (for which we have not yet created an image and so we will also be creating an image for the MongoDB data store).

Replication and clustering

While the detailed discussion on this topic is beyond the scope of this book, it makes logical sense to briefly look at what these mean before we get into the nitty gritty of configuring the two using Trove.

Please do remember that this is a general understanding and certain advanced features provided by some database engines may follow a different pattern.

Replication

Replication defined in the simplest terms is the process of keeping a copy of the data available on another node. Replication typically has two or more nodes, where one is the master (where reads and writes happen) and the others are slaves (where only reads can happen). There are concepts of master-master replication, but that's beyond the scope of this book.

There are two main reasons/benefits for which one could opt for replication:

- For failover (Business Continuity Plan):
    - In the event the master fails, the slave can be promoted and the applications can continue to work
    - The failover is mostly manual, but can be automated with scripts
    - There can be consistency issues with the data as replication of the data is a timed activity and there could be a possibility of data loss with the master

- For performance improvement:
    - In order to share the load of data reads (for reports), slaves could serve the purpose
    - In such scenarios, masters are used for database writes and real-time data reads, while slaves can be used for near real-time data reads

Clustering

Clustering focusses on a single-point agenda, *Availability*. Clustering is available at various levels from hardware clusters to operating system clusters to application clusters. However, in terms of databases, a cluster ensures that the *atomicity* of the transaction is only completed when the data is written on all the nodes.

Clusters are used where high availability is desired without any loss of data.

Replication in Trove

Replication is natively available to most of the relational database engines. However, the methods that might be used to replicate data may vary from database engine to database engine. There might be a possibility that more than one method may be available for a database engine.

As we already know, this is also based on the concept of strategies, so let's take a look at the various strategies available for replication.

 Replication uses the Trove backup/restore to set up the initial data transfer from the master to the slave. So, if Swift is unavailable or backup is not configured, this feature will not be operational.

Supported data stores

At the time of writing this book, the following data stores and their methods are supported for replication:

Data store name	Strategy name	Replication strategy class name
MySQL	MysqlBinlogReplication	trove.trove.guestagent. strategies.replication.mysql_ binlog
MySQL/ Percona	MysqlGTIDReplication	trove.trove.guestagent. strategies.replication.mysql_ gtid
MySQL/ Percona/ MariaDB	MysqlReplicationBase	trove.trove.guestagent. strategies.replication.mysql_ base

Data store name	Strategy name	Replication strategy class name
MariaDB	MariaDBGTIDReplication	trove.trove.guestagent. strategies.replication. experimental.mariadb_gtid
Redis	RedisSyncReplication	trove.trove.guestagent. strategies.replication. experimental.redis_sync

MySQL base strategies can also be used for its variants like Percona and MariaDB. GTID-based replication was introduced in MySQL version 5.6. MariaDB also introduced GTID-based replication, but it was not compatible with MySQL and Percona. Therefore, Trove implemented another class for MariaDB GTID implementation as seen from the previous table.

As we already know, strategies are implemented in the guest agent, and therefore, we can also plug our own strategies if your enterprise has a different mechanism or we want to enable it for a data store that has not yet been implemented.

The classes that are implemented for any replication to work are:

- `get_master_reference`: Provides the reference to the master node
- `snapshot_for_replication`: Captures a snapshot of the master database
- `enable_as_master`: Configure to act as master
- `enable_as_slave`: Configure to act as slave
- `detach_slave`: Detach the slave from the master
- `demote_master`: Switch off replication from the master node

The current implementation supports only master-slave, where the slave is populated asynchronously and is read only.

Setting up replications

Setting up a replica works in the same way backup and restore works due to the concept of strategies; however, for the sake of clarity of understanding, let us take a look at the process.

We cannot attach a currently running instance as a replica of another running instance. Replication is only done when we create an instance in Trove as a replica of the master.

The high-level process is as follows:

- User requests a replica of an already running Trove database
- A backup of the existing database is taken
- Another instance is created using the same backup

Replication is established.

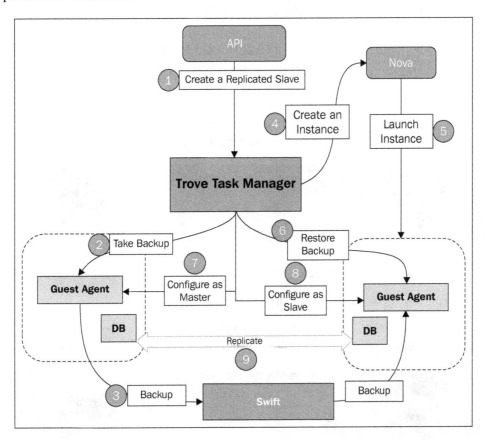

The order is not strictly sequential, and some of them happen in parallel.

Creating a replicated pair

In this example, we will create a replication of an already existing MySQL database. The command format is very much `trove create` with the `-replica_of` (and optionally `replica-count` to create more than one replica) parameter passed to it. The parameter will need the ID of the Trove instance, so we will execute the `trove list` command to get that.

To show the replication, we will create a replication master using the `trove create` command as follows (you may choose to ignore this and just create a replica of an already running instance, but we will create a new one for the purpose of this book).

```
trove create repl-master 2 --size 1 --datastore mysql \
--datastore_version 5.6
```

Once the master is ready, we can extract its ID (looking at the `trove list` command), as we will need it for the next command.

```
+--------------+-------------+-----------+-------------------+--------+-----------+------+
| ID           | Name        | Datastore | Datastore Version | Status | Flavor ID | Size |
+--------------+-------------+-----------+-------------------+--------+-----------+------+
| 0d42cc11-... | repl-master | mysql     | 5.6               | ACTIVE | 2         |    1 |
| c8dbde65-... | mysql_gui   | mysql     | 5.6               | ACTIVE | 2         |    1 |
+--------------+-------------+-----------+-------------------+--------+-----------+------+
```

The ID is **0d42cc11-a2df-499f-9b25-5dfdaf597fab** (the screenshot has been snipped).

We will create a replica using the command:

```
trove create repl-slave 2 --size 1 --datastore mysql \
--datastore_version 5.6 --replica_of 0d42cc11-a2df-499f-9b25-5dfdaf597fab
```

```
alokas@DevStack:/etc/trove$ trove create repl-slave 2 --size 1 --datastore mysql \
> --datastore_version 5.6 --replica_of 0d42cc11-a2df-499f-9b25-5dfdaf597fab
+-------------------+--------------------------------------+
| Property          | Value                                |
+-------------------+--------------------------------------+
| created           | 2016-02-01T16:58:09                  |
| datastore         | mysql                                |
| datastore_version | 5.6                                  |
| flavor            | 2                                    |
| id                | 51ede63f-9a93-4b8b-a5fb-28e9b5e06632 |
| name              | repl-slave                           |
| replica_of        | 0d42cc11-a2df-499f-9b25-5dfdaf597fab |
| status            | BUILD                                |
| updated           | 2016-02-01T16:58:09                  |
| volume            | 1                                    |
+-------------------+--------------------------------------+
```

If we execute the `trove list` command, we will see that the master database will be in the state of **BACKUP** and the slave will be in the **BUILD** state as expected.

```
alokas@DevStack:/etc/trove$ trove list
+------------+-------------+-----------+-------------------+--------+-----------+------+
| ID         | Name        | Datastore | Datastore Version | Status | Flavor ID | Size |
+------------+-------------+-----------+-------------------+--------+-----------+------+
| 0d42cc11-..| repl-master | mysql     | 5.6               | BACKUP | 2         |    1 |
| 51ede63f-..| repl-slave  | mysql     | 5.6               | BUILD  | 2         |    1 |
| c8dbde65-..| mysql_gui   | mysql     | 5.6               | ACTIVE | 2         |    1 |
+------------+-------------+-----------+-------------------+--------+-----------+------+
```

We will wait for the replica to be active before verifying the replication. The configuration for the replicated slave is controlled by the file present in the templates folder as seen earlier in *Chapter 6, Configuring the Trove Instances*.

In our case, `replica.config.template` and `replica_source.config.template` are used for the slave and master respectively.

```
alokas@DevStack:/opt/stack/trove/trove/templates/mysql$ cat replica.config.template
[mysqld]
log_bin = /var/lib/mysql/data/mysql-bin.log
relay_log = /var/lib/mysql/data/mysql-relay-bin.log
relay_log_info_repository = TABLE
relay_log_recovery = 1
relay_log_purge = 1
log_slave_updates = ON
enforce_gtid_consistency = ON
gtid_mode = ON
read_only = true
alokas@DevStack:/opt/stack/trove/trove/templates/mysql$ cat replica_source.config.template
[mysqld]
log_bin = /var/lib/mysql/data/mysql-bin.log
binlog_format = MIXED
enforce_gtid_consistency = ON
gtid_mode = ON
log_slave_updates = ON
alokas@DevStack:/opt/stack/trove/trove/templates/mysql$
```

Verifying replication

Replication can be verified by making some modifications to the primary (master) and ensuring that the modifications also propagate back to the slave node.

We will create a database called `testdb` on the master by using the `database-create` command.

```
trove database-create 0d42cc11-a2df-499f-9b25-5dfdaf597fab testdb
```

This will create the database on the master, but since the slave is replicated, we can execute a `database-list` command for the slave, and **testdb** will also show up on both the nodes.

```
alokas@DevStack:/etc/trove$ trove database-list 51ede63f-9a93-4b8b-a5fb-28e9b5e06632
+---------+
| Name    |
+---------+
| testdb  |
+---------+
```

We can log in and also check that the replication is indeed configured.

 Please note that the replication is only from the master to the slave; any changes to the slave will not be replicated back to the master. This is by design of MySQL replication and is not controlled by Trove.

Trove has no role to play in this process after it sets up the initial replication and hence we won't be talking about the understanding of MySQL replication itself as it is beyond the scope of this book.

Trove can, however, perform some failover functions in the replication that it has set up. We will take a look at that in the next section.

Failover options

We will take a look at the basic functions that Trove can perform when it comes to failover:

- Detach replica (`detach-replica`)
  - This breaks replication permanently and is an irreversible action. Please remember that Trove can only create a new replica; it cannot set an already existing instance as the replication slave.
  - This can be used as a point in time snapshot, to have another version of the database.

- Promote to replication master (`promote-to-replica-source`)
  - This replaces the current (running) master with a new master

- Eject the master (`eject-replica-source`)
  - This essentially is used to eject an already failed master to establish a new master

In order to show the appropriate working of these commands, we will create another replica of the same source (`repl-master`). We will execute another `trove create` command.

```
trove create repl-slave2 2 --size 1 --datastore mysql \
  --datastore_version 5.6 \
  --replica_of 0d42cc11-a2df-499f-9b25-5dfdaf597fab
```

This will create a second replica called `repl-slave2`; we will wait for this to be active as well.

We will execute the `trove show <instance name/ ID>` command to see all the replicas that are available.

```
alokas@DevStack:/opt/stack/logs$ trove list
+-------------+--------------+-----------+-------------------+--------+-----------+------+
| ID          | Name         | Datastore | Datastore Version | Status | Flavor ID | Size |
+-------------+--------------+-----------+-------------------+--------+-----------+------+
| 0d42cc11-.. | repl-master  | mysql     | 5.6               | ACTIVE | 2         |    1 |
| 51ede63f-.. | repl-slave   | mysql     | 5.6               | ACTIVE | 2         |    1 |
| ab18c2c8-.. | repl-slave2  | mysql     | 5.6               | ACTIVE | 2         |    1 |
+-------------+--------------+-----------+-------------------+--------+-----------+------+
alokas@DevStack:/opt/stack/logs$
alokas@DevStack:/opt/stack/logs$ trove show repl-master
+-------------------+--------------------------------------------------------------------------+
| Property          | Value                                                                    |
+-------------------+--------------------------------------------------------------------------+
| created           | 2016-02-01T01:46:36                                                      |
| datastore         | mysql                                                                    |
| datastore_version | 5.6                                                                      |
| flavor            | 2                                                                        |
| id                | 0d42cc11-a2df-499f-9b25-5dfdaf597fab                                     |
| ip                | 10.1.10.3                                                                |
| name              | repl-master                                                              |
| replicas          | 51ede63f-9a93-4b8b-a5fb-28e9b5c06632, ab18c2c8-fd52-4198-b4d0-1d204806f776 |
| status            | ACTIVE                                                                   |
| updated           | 2016-02-01T01:46:58                                                      |
| volume            | 1                                                                        |
| volume_used       | 0.1                                                                      |
+-------------------+--------------------------------------------------------------------------+
```

As we can see, the Trove instance called `repl-master` has two replicas listed. We can verify that the newly created replica also has the database that we created on the master (testdb).

```
trove database-list ab18c2c8-fd52-4198-b4d0-1d204806f776
```

You should see that the database exists.

Promote to the replica master

We can promote any of the databases to the master, and the state of that database should be copied over.

Say, for instance, we create a database called `testdb12` on `repl-slave` using the following command:

```
trove database-create 51ede63f-9a93-4b8b-a5fb-28e9b5e06632 testdb12
```

This database will only be available in the `repl-slave` instance and will not be replicated, as the current replicated source is `repl-master`. So if we check the database-list on the other nodes, they won't list testdb12.

Now, if we promote the instance `repl-slave` to the replica master, for, say, taking down the master for maintenance, we will execute the command `trove promote-to-replica-source <instance name/id>`.

```
trove promote-to-replica-source repl-slave
```

Once this command is executed, the status of all the instances will be set to **PROMOTE** and Trove will work its magic; we will wait for all of them to come back to **ACTIVE**.

```
alokas@DevStack:/opt/stack/logs$ trove list
+-------------+-------------+-----------+-------------------+---------+-----------+------+
| ID          | Name        | Datastore | Datastore Version | Status  | Flavor ID | Size |
+-------------+-------------+-----------+-------------------+---------+-----------+------+
| 0d42cc11-...| repl-master | mysql     | 5.6               | PROMOTE | 2         | 1    |
| 51ede63f-...| repl-slave  | mysql     | 5.6               | PROMOTE | 2         | 1    |
| ab18c2c8-...| repl-slave2 | mysql     | 5.6               | PROMOTE | 2         | 1    |
+-------------+-------------+-----------+-------------------+---------+-----------+------+
alokas@DevStack:/opt/stack/logs$
```

It will also replicate `testdb12` to the other nodes as a side effect. Hence, executing the `database-list` command on `repl-slave2` as shown next will now list **testdb** and **testdb12**:

```
trove database-list ab18c2c8-fd52-4198-b4d0-1d204806f776
```

```
alokas@DevStack:/opt/stack/logs$ trove database-list ab18c2c8-
+----------+
| Name     |
+----------+
| testdb   |
| testdb12 |
+----------+
```

Please use this method to take the master into account. Also, remember that this doesn't handle the application connections to the databases. In a production environment, if we were to do this, then the DNS record must be changed to ensure that the applications write to the correct master server.

This method also swaps the public IPs (floating IP address) of the servers if they are available. This method allows the master to maintain the same public IP address and the applications can keep connecting to the same IP address.

There is a blueprint at `https://blueprints.launchpad.net/trove/+spec/barbican-integration` to enable Barbican integration for DNS changes in the roadmap.

Eject the master

This should be only done in a failed master scenario. This command can only be executed in the current master (at this point, the instance `repl-slave` is the master of the replication group) and only if the master is not responding. These safeguards are coded into the Trove system to prevent accidental ejections.

This command ejects the current master and then forces a re-election for the new master. The new master is effectively the one with the most current replica of the old master.

In order to simulate this, let us turn off the current master `repl-slave` by simply killing the guest agent as shown in the following screenshot:

```
alokas@DevStack:/opt/stack/logs$ ssh ubuntu@10.1.10.4  i ~/.ssh/id_rsa
Welcome to Ubuntu 14.04.3 LTS (GNU/Linux 3.13.0-76-generic i686)

 * Documentation:  https://help.ubuntu.com/

   Get cloud support with Ubuntu Advantage Cloud Guest:
     http://www.ubuntu.com/business/services/cloud

Last login: Tue Feb  2 06:07:59 2016 from 10.1.10.1

ubuntu@repl-slave:~$
ubuntu@repl-slave:~$
ubuntu@repl-slave:~$ sudo su
root@repl-slave:/home/ubuntu#
root@repl-slave:/home/ubuntu# ps -ef | grep trove | awk '{print $2}' | xargs kill -9
root@repl-slave:/home/ubuntu#
```

This will kill the heartbeat that the guest agent sends and emulates a server-down scenario.

We will now execute the command:

```
trove eject-replica-source repl-slave
```

This will remove **repl-slave** as the master, change the status to **EJECT**, and force the election of the new master.

```
alokas@DevStack:/opt/stack/trove/trove$ trove list
+-----------------+--------------+-----------+-------------------+--------+-----------+------+
| ID              | Name         | Datastore | Datastore Version | Status | Flavor ID | Size |
+-----------------+--------------+-----------+-------------------+--------+-----------+------+
| 0d42cc11-....   | repl-master  | mysql     | 5.6               | EJECT  | 2         |    1 |
| 51ede63f-....   | repl-slave   | mysql     | 5.6               | EJECT  | 2         |    1 |
| ab18c2c8-....   | repl-slave2  | mysql     | 5.6               | EJECT  | 2         |    1 |
+-----------------+--------------+-----------+-------------------+--------+-----------+------+
```

Once it transitions back to active, we will quickly execute the `show` command and see what happened.

```
alokas@DevStack:/opt/stack/trove/trove$ trove show repl-master | grep repli
| replicas         | ab18c2c8-fd52-4198-b4d0-1d204806f776 |
alokas@DevStack:/opt/stack/trove/trove$ trove show repl-slave | grep repli
alokas@DevStack:/opt/stack/trove/trove$
alokas@DevStack:/opt/stack/trove/trove$ trove show repl-slave2 | grep repli
| replica_of       | 0d42cc11-a2df-499f-9b25-5dfdaf597fab |
alokas@DevStack:/opt/stack/trove/trove$
```

As we can see, **repl-master** got elected the new master as it has the replicas in the output. **repl-slave2** remained a slave (note the **replica_of** output); the recently ejected master **repl-slave** is now an independent database. Please note that even when the server comes up, none of the other servers will point to it and replicate from it.

Detach replica

Detach replica is to remove replication between the source and the replica. This step cannot be revoked and this creates a point in time snapshot.

Say we want to now finally break away `repl-slave2` from our replication group, so that all the servers are now independent; we can execute the command:

```
trove detach-replica repl-slave2
```

This will detach the replica from its master. Another use case for doing this will be a dev/test environment, where a database is created and populated with test data, and then the replica can be disconnected to work on the database without impacting the base data.

We should also remember that we cannot delete a master database until any of the replicas exist, so we will need to use this command to detach the replicas before the master can be deleted.

Clustering in Trove

This is also implemented by the use of strategies, but unlike in the case of replication that is a guest agent strategy alone, the strategy for clustering comprises a strategy for `trove-api`, `trove-taskmanager`, and `trove-guestagent`.

This is due to the contrast among different database engines in the way they implement clustering. Having said that, Trove in this case also is purely an enabler and the database engine itself has to support clustering for Trove to even consider implementing a strategy.

Supported data store

The Juno release brought clustering to MongoDB, and now with the current release, we have clustering enabled for the following data stores and the associated actions that are supported:

Data store name	Cluster actions supported
MongoDB	Create/add shards/grow/shrink/delete
PXC	Create/delete/grow/shrink
Redis	Create/delete
Vertica	Create/delete

As we can see, MongoDB has more features when it comes to clustering in Trove compared to its counterparts; we will use that to test clustering.

Please remember that we don't have a MongoDB image, so we either create our own like shown in the previous chapters, or we can download the image from the Tarballs site. Please remember that the IP range needs to be 10.0.0.0/24 if we need to use images downloaded from the website.

Since we don't have the image, we will use DIB to create a new image using the following command. Please remember to export the variables before running the command (as shown in *Chapter 5, Provisioning Database Instances*).

Creating and uploading the MongoDB image

The command to build the MongoDB image is shown as follows:

```
cd /opt/stack


diskimage-builder/bin/disk-image-create -a i386 \
-o /home/alokas/images/ubuntu_mongo/ubuntu_mongodb -x \
--qemu-img-options compat=0.10 ubuntu vm heat-cfntools \
cloud-init-datasources ubuntu-guest ubuntu-mongodb
```

We will then upload the image to Glance.

```
glance image-create --name mongodb --disk-format qcow2 \
 --container-format bare \
 --visibility public \
 --file /home/alokas/images/ubuntu_mongo/ubuntu_mongodb.qcow2
```

We will have to note down the ID of the image in the output of the previous command. We will then create the data store and the data store version.

```
trove-manage datastore_update mongodb ''


trove-manage datastore_version_update mongodb 2.4.9 \
 mongodb 0b446ab8-5c35-44eb-902c-d3b040d03296 mongodb 1
```

Once the MongoDB image is ready, we will need to create a suitable flavor for MongoDB, which we can do by executing the command `nova flavor-create` by passing the flavor ID (please ensure the flavor ID is not already taken by using the command `nova flavor-list`. In this case, we have used 6 as that was not used; we specify the RAM to be 1024 MB or 1 GB and 4 GB disk).

```
nova flavor-create mongodb.fl 6 1024 4 1
```

```
alokas@DevStack:/opt/stack$ nova flavor-create mongodb.fl 6 1024 4 1
+----+------------+-----------+------+-----------+------+-------+-------------+-----------+
| ID | Name       | Memory_MB | Disk | Ephemeral | Swap | VCPUs | RXTX_Factor | Is_Public |
+----+------------+-----------+------+-----------+------+-------+-------------+-----------+
| 6  | mongodb.fl | 1024      | 4    | 0         |      | 1     | 1.0         | True      |
+----+------------+-----------+------+-----------+------+-------+-------------+-----------+
```

Creating a cluster

Understanding the sharded clustering concepts in MongoDB is beyond the scope of this book; however, from a very basic point of view, the MongoDB cluster has three components:

- Replica sets
- Configuration servers
- Query routers

The replica sets are a group of MongoDB processes that keep the same information (replication that we discussed earlier). The query router is used to route the queries to appropriate replica sets/shards. The configuration server stores the metadata for the shards.

The reason it is recommended to have an odd number of servers in a replica set is that we will always have voting ability and will be able to elect a primary node.

A simplified diagram to show the whole process of clustering is next. The replicated set keep the data replicated among themselves and the query router and the configuration server directs the query to the correct node. Please note that with a single replica set, there is no sharding shown in the diagram.

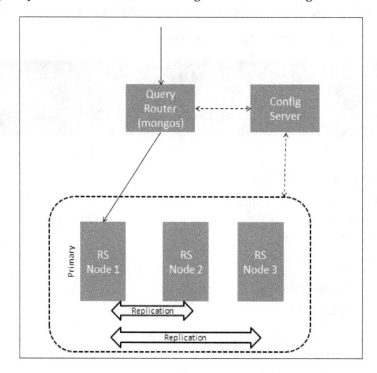

We can then create the MongoDB three-node cluster using the following command:

```
trove cluster-create mongo-cl --datastore mongodb \
--datastore_version 2.4.9 \
--instance flavor_id=6,volume=4 \
--instance flavor_id=6,volume=4 \
--instance flavor_id=6,volume=4
```

Please note that the MongoDB cluster needs a minimum of three nodes (to ensure the replicated set has the ability to elect a master). At the time of writing this book, only a three-node cluster is supported. However, in the future, a three, five, or seven-node cluster may be supported.

Please note that the cluster is not viewable by the generic `trove list` command. In order to view the cluster, we have to execute the `trove cluster-list` command and see that the cluster is created. The cluster is considered ready for use, when the **Task Name** in the cluster-list output task is set to **NONE** as shown in the following screenshot:

```
alokas@DevStack:/opt/stack/trove/trove$ trove cluster-list
+----------------+-----------+-----------+-------------------+-----------+
| ID             | Name      | Datastore | Datastore Version | Task Name |
+----------------+-----------+-----------+-------------------+-----------+
| c070435f-....  | mongo-cl  | mongodb   | 2.4.9             | NONE      |
+----------------+-----------+-----------+-------------------+-----------+
```

In order to see the cluster members, we use the command `trove cluster-instance <ClusterName>`. So, in our case, the command will be:

`trove cluster-instance mongo-cl`

```
+----------------+------------------+-----------+------+
| ID             | Name             | Flavor ID | Size |
+----------------+------------------+-----------+------+
| 37487948-....  | mongo-cl-rs1-1   | 10        | 4    |
| c20b9dfc-....  | mongo-cl-rs1-2   | 10        | 4    |
| c4b3432e-....  | mongo-cl-rs1-3   | 10        | 4    |
+----------------+------------------+-----------+------+
```

The configuration server and query router are also spun up, which should be seen in the output of the `nova list` command.

```
alokas@DevStack:/opt/stack/trove/trove$ nova list
+---------------+---------------------+--------+------------+-------------+----------------------+
| ID            | Name                | Status | Task State | Power State | Networks             |
+---------------+---------------------+--------+------------+-------------+----------------------+
| 0da80b8a-...  | mongo-cl-configsvr-1| ACTIVE | -          | Running     | private=10.1.10.4    |
| 432fd3d3-...  | mongo-cl-mongos-1   | ACTIVE | -          | Running     | private=10.1.10.5    |
| 37487948-.... | mongo-cl-rs1-1      | ACTIVE | -          | Running     | private=10.1.10.7    |
| c20b9dfc-.... | mongo-cl-rs1-2      | ACTIVE | -          | Running     | private=10.1.10.6    |
| c4b3432e-.... | mongo-cl-rs1-3      | ACTIVE | -          | Running     | private=10.1.10.8    |
+---------------+---------------------+--------+------------+-------------+----------------------+
```

Summary

The Trove system, when set up properly, can ease administration overheads, reduce wait time for database instances, and help the DBA to focus their energies on performing tasks such as query optimization.

Some of the benefits you can offer your enterprises by implementing Trove are enforce security, compliance, and best practices – since provisioning and management are highly automated, Trove is the best mechanism to implement security and enterprise-wide best practices practically at no cost. With Trove, you can choose the database of your choice depending on the use case and yet manage them seamlessly. And then we have agility – faster provisioning that helps you innovate at a faster rate and improved turnaround times for support.

We hope that this book helped you with the fundamental skills that are required for you to kickstart your Trove learning and wish you a successful *Database as Service* journey.

Index

parameter, adding 112
patching 109
removing 111
updating 110, 111
verification 106, 107, 111, 112
viewing 107, 108

J

Juno release
  about 14
  reference 15

K

Kilo release
  about 14
  reference 15

L

Liberty release
  about 14
  reference 15

M

multi-datastore scenario 9-11

N

Nova 83

O

OpenStack
  deploying methods 42-44
OpenStack services 44
OpenStack Trove
  about 1, 4
  architecture 5
  features 14
  installing 46

installing, from source 46-48
installing, with Ubuntu OpenStack
    repository 48, 49
terminology 7
OpenStack with Ansible
  reference 43
OpenStack with Chef
  reference 43
OpenStack with Fuel
  reference 43
OpenStack with Juju
  reference 43
OpenStack with PackStack
  reference 43
OpenStack with Puppet
  reference 43

P

packages
  corkscrew 22
  git 22
  screen 22
prerequisites, database instance
  datastore 80
  datastore versions 80
  flavors 80
prerequisites, DevStack
  installing 21
  packages, installing 22
  user, adding 21

Q

QCOW2 images, modifying with guestfish
  about 75
  commands, sending to guestfish 77
  files, modifying 76
  guestfish, installing 76
  images, loading 76
  user, adding to Ubuntu QCOW2 image 77

www.ingramcontent.com/pod-product-compliance
Lightning Source LLC
Chambersburg PA
CBHW060138060326
40690CB00018B/3920